The
OneTEAM Method™

by

PETER STROHKORB

DEDICATION

This book is dedicated to all hard-working professionals in sales and marketing roles everywhere. After all, without you no business could exist. May we together create a world where Sales and Marketing live in collaborative harmony, where we support each other to be the best that we can be, so that we will be recognized for our efforts and earn the respect and admiration of everyone.

TABLE OF CONTENTS

"Never mind a book about how to change myself.
I need a book about making everyone else change."

Peter Strohkorb

ACKNOWLEDGMENTS

This book would not have been possible to write without input from a number of specialists in their field. My heartfelt thanks go out to them for their generous insight and kind support:

Anoushka Gungadin, CEO at The Duke of Edinburgh's International Awards, Australia

Barbara Perzanowski, Chief Needle Mover at Move the Needle LLC, USA

Bob Hayward, Head of the Asia Pacific Centre of Excellence for IT Leaders at KPMG

Chris Glenister, Senior Account Executive at Telstra, Australia

Chuck Carey, CEO at Compendian Inc, USA

Craig Rispin, Business Futurist & Innovation Expert, Global

Daniel Sutic, Program Marketing Manager at Rackspace, Australia

Denis Preston, Recruitment Strategy Coach at True Colours People Solutions, Australia

Dr David Cooke, Managing Director at Konica Minolta Business Solutions Australia

Erin Mikan, APJ Marketing Manager - Global Systems Integrators at Dell, Australia

Gerhard Gschwandtner, Founder and CEO at Selling Power Magazine, USA

Jayson Darby, Psychology Project Coordinator at Thomas International, United Kingdom

John Bedwany, CEO at The Database Department, Australia

John Dougan, Client Director - Sales Strategy at Huthwaite, Australia

Jonathan Rubinsztein, CEO at UXC Red Rock Consulting, Australia

Kit Andrews, Business and Market Intelligence Analyst at RMIT University, Australia

ACKNOWLEDGMENTS ...CONTINUED

Lee Styger, Director MBA Program at Sydney Business School, Australia

Michael Cannon, CEO at The Silver Bullet Group, USA

Michael Doran, CEO, Business Psychs, Australia

Michael Shepherd, Director Sales & Marketing at Thales, Australia

Mitchell Filby, CEO at First Rock Consulting, Australia

Peter Wilson, CEO at Clarius Group, Australia

Ray Kloss, Head of Marketing Asia Pacific & Japan at SAP, Australia

Richard Nott, Program Manager - Finance & Business Transformation at Cochlear, Australia

Scott Kardash, Vice President Consulting at CGI, Australia

Scott Mason, Vice President of Marketing at Optus, Australia

Sonia Eland, Vice President Digital Alliances Eco-system at CSC, Australia

Suchi Pathak, Head of Psychology at Thomas International, UK

Toby Marshall, CEO at Lead Creation Pty Ltd, Australia

Ute Diversi, Senior Learning & Development Performance Management Specialist at Australian Government

Special thanks go to:

Vanessa Strohkorb, my long-suffering wife, for her enduring patience and loving support

John Michell for his kind hospitality and sanctuary

Bryan Szabo my excellent and very supportive editor

Paul and Linda Croft for their technical expertise and for squeezing my jobs into their busy schedules

Sandra Fernandez my very clever graphic designer

Peter Strohkorb
CONSULTING

Dear Reader,

Thank you for your interest in this book. It was a labor of love and passion for me, and I am pleased to present it to you here.

I invite you to find out more about the OneTEAM Method™ and what it can do both for you and for your organization.

Please feel free to contact us at

www.peterstrohkorbconsulting.com

I look forward to working with you.

CEO
Peter Strohkorb Consulting International

Introduction

The world of sales and marketing is changing. Bain & Company summed up the changing landscape and what it means for the future of sales very aptly in a 2014 report, "Mastering The New Reality of Sales":

- The line between sales and marketing will disappear; an integrated "smarketing" function will emerge to synchronize coverage and resources with target customers.

- Selling costs will grow faster than revenue without a deliberate effort to reverse creeping complexity and administrative burden.

- Prospects will have screened you out of consideration based on your digital footprint (or its absence) even before one of your representatives has a chance to understand their needs.

- Your customers will spend more time analyzing your offerings than you will on analytics to understand their buying behavior.

- A competitor will offer your customers better, more seamless service through lower-touch, lower-cost channels, winning share and loyalty.

- You will be forced to either retrain or turn over more than half of your reps to keep up with competitor sellers who truly add value rather than just communicate features and take orders.

Source: "Mastering The New Reality of Sales" by "Dianne Ledingham, Mark Kovac, Laura Beaudin and Sarah Dey Burton, Bain & Company, http://www.bain.com/publications/articles/mastering-the-new-reality-of-sales.aspx

It seems that many large organizations are finding adapting to these changes and others like them a daily challenge. Even worse, they often are hamstrung by short-term decision-making, shrinking budgets and entrenched perceptions and attitudes. As a result, many organizations are seeking ways to enable more effective collaboration between their sales and marketing teams, but they address this objective with Band-Aid solutions that just don't seem to deliver lasting business benefits. The new trend is a movement away from supporting the heroic efforts of a small number of individuals and towards a focus on integrated teamwork.

I call this new focus and the method that produces it Sales+Marketing Collaboration.

Sales+Marketing Collaboration responds to a series of all-too-common business problems:

Problems:

Missed sales targets, wasted time, effort and money on both sides, Marketing creating content and sales leads that are not utilized by the sales team, sales reps creating their own marketing content instead of selling, all the above resulting in frustration about each team's (perceived or actual) lack of respect for, and support of, the other.

Causes:

Sales and marketing teams are collaborating poorly, or not at all. National marketing and sales teams only meet a few times per year.

Mutual understanding is sorely lacking, mutual respect rare, and therefore collaborative results are either disappointing or non-existent.

Solution:

Establish a consistent and bi-directional feedback loop between Sales and Marketing that embraces their interactions *in toto*, not just the qualification of Marketing's sales leads.

Let's investigate this subject further.

Most business executives instinctively understand how Sales/Marketing misalignment can be hugely wasteful. I have seen marketing people produce sales collateral, campaigns, leads, white papers, thought leadership pieces and other sales support material only to watch, helpless and frustrated, from the sidelines as salespeople completely ignore this material.

With the shoe on the other foot, I have watched as under-supported sales reps, in large part thanks to this lack of support from Marketing, create their own content, thereby essentially doubling up on Marketing's work, instead of focusing on what they're really good at, i.e. selling.

As if this wasteful state of affairs is not bad enough, the Internet and the evolving Buyer's Journey (which we'll examine in detail later) have exacerbated the situation. Thanks to increasingly information-savvy buyers, your sales reps are no longer in the driving seat; increasingly, they have become merely a passenger in the sales process.

This new paradigm means that Sales and Marketing now need to work together more closely than they ever have before in order to capture the buyer's attention early. Organizations that ignore this trend hand their innovative and nimble competitors an uneven advantage.

In today's marketplace, effective Sales+Marketing Collaboration can make the difference between success and failure. The degree to which your organization collaborates, or does not collaborate, is a leading indicator of how well – or how poorly – your organization is equipped to cope with the new buying style. Our own research, as well as that of

many highly regarded third parties, shows that the organizations that possess the most up-to-date and powerful collaboration methods and tools are those that will best be able to translate their collective efforts into short- and long-term business success. I will elaborate on this research and on our solutions a little later.

Chapter 1:
Who Says there is a Problem?

In 2006, three eminent, internationally recognized experts, Philip Kotler, Neil Rackham and Suj Krishnaswamy, joined forces to publish an article in the Harvard Business Review called "Ending the War between Sales and Marketing"*. As their strongly worded title suggests, they, like me, recognize the perilous state of collaboration between sales and marketing departments in large organizations. But, of course, sales and marketing people are only human. Nobody wants to shoulder the blame for less-than-ideal sales performance. Mea culpas are few and far between in those departments that are most responsible for driving the financial engine of organizations, namely Sales and Marketing. There is, however, plenty of blame to go around.

Here are some troubling statistics gathered from around the global sales and marketing research community:

"67% of sales professionals do not achieve their personal sales quota." (The TAS Group)

"60% of sales pipeline is stuck with no decision pending." (Sales Benchmark Index)

"Only 25% of sales leads and collateral that Marketing creates is ever used by Sales teams." (IDC)

CSO Insights says that
"Less than 35% of a sales rep's time is spent on selling."

"Less than 35% of a sales rep's time is spent on selling." (CSO Insights)

"Almost 78% of newly hired sales reps take 6 months or longer to become fully proficient at selling." (Accenture)

"Over 30 percent of sales reps spend between 20 and 50 percent of their precious selling time looking for, creating or modifying Marketing content." (Peter Strohkorb Consulting International)

This dismal state of affairs is costing organizations more than you might think.

Our own research, and my personal experience found that over one third of sales reps spend between 20% and 50% of their precious selling time searching for the right sales collateral. 1.58% of those surveyed said they spend more than half their time looking for the right Marketing material.

Even if we round that up to 2%, it doesn't sound like an alarming number, but I think we can all agree that it should be 0%, and no higher. No, i.e. zero, salesperson should be compelled to so waste his or her productive time that half of it is spent doing something that should take almost no time at all. What a waste, what inefficiency, what

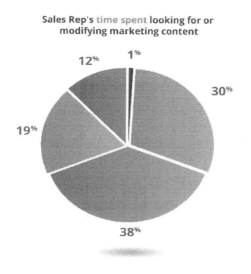

Sales Rep's time spent looking for or modifying marketing content

missed opportunities, and what a waste of money. No matter how you try to justify this, it seems hard to believe that this sort of inefficiency would be tolerated in today's efficiency-driven business climate.

Clearly, there is (and long has been) a crisis of sorts in the sales world, one that coincides with something of a collaborative crisis. Since 2008, slowing markets have been the culprit du jour for the former, but the latest research and the realities of the new digital economy show that collaborative enterprizes, i.e. the ones that ensure through good communication, shared metrics and processes that Sales and Marketing are working in unison, are the ones that are recovering the quickest and outstripping their competitors in the new race to the top.

The inverse is also true: those that are collaborating ineffectively or not at all are losing ground by the minute to their more collaborative competitors. For many of these organizations, denial and a fundamental blindness to the root causes of stagnant or declining revenues are keeping them from the kind of success that more collaborative enterprizes are enjoying.

If a Sales/Marketing partnership is the goal (and it should be), these root causes need to be recognized for the business impeders they really are. A mutual disconnect often causes cycles of blame and credit-taking, preventing both sides from recognizing that the problems they are facing are collective. Unfortunately, blaming the other side for sales failures is commonplace in organizations with poor Sales/Marketing alignment. When not meeting sales quotas, Sales is quick to point a finger at Marketing, saying that the leads are no good, that the collateral is of insufficient quality or that the prices set by Marketing are too high. Marketing, as might be expected, points the finger right back at Sales, saying that their poor execution is to blame. Sales may claim that Marketing has no real appreciation for the subtle interactions between salespeople and their customers. Marketing on the other hand may insist that the sales force is incompetent, short-term focused, or unable to understand brand building and the bigger market picture. Watch, though, how quickly assigning blame turns to taking credit when famine turns to feast.

Make no mistake, the largest problem facing would-be collaborators is this cycle of blame and the overwhelmingly vitriolic nature of the Sales vs. Marketing relationship that it produces. Matthew Dixon and Brent Adamson, commenting on a recent Corporate Executive Board survey of several hundred sales and marketing professionals, noted that "a full 87%" of the comments that passed back and forth when Sales was asked about Marketing and vice versa "were negative".

In a 2004/2005 study, MathMarketing surveyed more than 1,400 professionals from 84 countries and found Sales/Marketing misalignment to be pandemic. This disconnect, they said, "can be heard in the corridors". A few examples of the kind of language they encountered:

What Marketing says about Sales:

"Sales doesn't follow up our leads."

"Sales is asking for a stand at the trade show, but I know this never works."

"Sales doesn't even seem to know what campaigns we are running."

What Sales says about Marketing:

"Marketing has no idea about the real world."

"Marketing costs money, Sales makes money"

"Marketing never produces enough leads, and their leads are rubbish anyway."

"Marketing spends so much money, but I have no idea what they do with it all."

I have heard this kind of language so often that it no longer surprises me. It is becoming increasingly obvious – and not just to me – that Sales/Marketing misalignment is one of the largest issues facing today's organizations.

Here are a few more examples:

Jonathan Rubinsztein is the CEO of UXC Red Rock Consulting, the largest Oracle Consulting business in Australia and New Zealand with 8 offices and over 600 staff. Jonathan is a dynamic and energetic leader who prides himself on being able to help grow businesses aggressively whilst maintaining each organization's distinct culture and that X-factor that separates them from their competition. Yet even he says: *"There is a gap between Sales and Marketing. The larger the organization, the larger the gap."*

I couldn't have put it better myself.

Chris Glenister, Business Development Executive at a very large telecommunications company, has also recognized just how pressing the issue is. He recently spoke in no uncertain terms about some of the symptoms of the sorry state of Sales+Marketing Collaboration that he has witnessed:

"One doesn't talk to the other, so you find a mix of Marketing pushing out campaigns and initiatives based on their own targets, product being pushed out due to holes in target, etc. As a rule, I have seen Marketing campaigns and information sent out with a sales rep's name and details at the bottom of the email, yet without them engaging with this salesperson first.

I also see product being pushed out via Marketing with no real thoughts as to how to position it in the market, how competitive is it against others and whether it is relevant to the customer.

Whilst Marketing continues to operate without the direct engagement of the Sales force they will continue to offer hit and miss initiatives.

Only when Marketing and Sales work together [...] will these two groups succeed."

From my own experience here are two more (very different) quotes that I hear in variations in my travels:

"What's the difference between a salesperson and a computer? You only have to punch the information into a computer once." (boom boom)

But also: "When Sales and Marketing are not working together, you have nothing." (hear hear)

Speaking of my personal experiences, when I attended a Sales and Marketing alignment conference in Chicago, USA in 2014, I met with the Sales VP of a regional bank. He told me a familiar story, namely that their marketing team sends out standardized letters in the mail to contacts on a prospect list in order to generate leads for the reps to follow up on.

Get this: even though the reps' name and contact details appear on the bottom of the letter, Marketing had never checked with the individual reps to ask their permission to use their names, or even just to get their buy-in.

And there was more. Marketing at this bank completely absolved itself from any of the commercial outcomes of their lead generation campaign. I asked the VP how the leads are handed over from Marketing to Sales. He looked at me as though the question were a strange one and said: "They aren't."

What seems to happen is that after Marketing sends the letters, they declare their job done and, from then on forward, it is up to the sales rep to respond to any enquiries that come to the rep directly (because their name and contact details were included at the bottom of the letters that Marketing was sending out).

Here's the kicker: Marketing has no idea whether, and to what degree, their mail out campaign works for the sales team. It seems that there is no formal feedback communication process in place whatsoever. This is a multi-100 million US dollar bank!

Imagine how much better they could perform if only there were a feedback loop in place that informs Marketing about what actually works for Sales, and what does not.

Then there is my personal favorite. I was sitting in on a sales meeting at the head office of a well-known global technology giant when a senior sales executive, speaking off the cuff, offered the following nugget: "Sales brings in the money and Marketing spends it. They should be working for us!"

What is painfully obvious in all this is the fact that neither side truly appreciates the other, perhaps because they don't really understand – at least not very well – what the other team does, or how they do it. Too often, they are accustomed to seeing the world of business through lenses that are ground and shaped by their personal experiences and limited perspectives. Often, sales and marketing departments are both guilty of celebrating narrowly defined successes that little reflect the overall financial health of the organization. These small successes turn into a shield of sort than can be used to deflect criticism that relates to their poor collaborative practices.

Here is the realization that stares organizations in the face the instant they stop trying to ignore the issue or deflect the blame for its causes: Sales and marketing teams, when they collaborate poorly, are harming not only themselves but the entire organization. Blame shifting and reluctance to adopt new (and quite often radically different) approaches has to stop, and this process begins with a simultaneous movement in both directions, top-down and bottom-up.

Chapter Takeaway

We looked briefly at the kind of disputes that commonly occur between Sales and Marketing in larger organizations (and sometimes even in smaller ones). So how do large or growing organizations prevent these kinds of disputes from arising, or, if they have already emerged, what can be done to reverse the trend? As with every journey, the first step is the most important one. The first step, as we shall see later, is recognizing that you have a problem.

Peter Strohkorb

Chapter 2:
Help is at Hand

The crisis is real, it is acute and it is ubiquitous. Looking at our own research as well as third-party insight, it is clear that the problem of poor Sales+Marketing Collaboration is pervasive mainly in larger organizations. It is in these larger organizations that poor collaboration can have profound ramifications on individuals and on the entire organizational culture. It is an issue that must be addressed if teamwork is to be sustained and success achieved.

As we will see in later chapters, my OneTEAM Method™ addresses all these points and offers a holistic solution to an all-too-familiar problem, namely that of Sales and Marketing not collaborating as well as they could.

While some organizations are forging ahead using outdated operational models, or are even ignoring the problem of Sales/Marketing misalignment altogether (often at their own peril), some forward-thinking organizations have attempted – or are attempting – to address the collaborative issues at the heart of their dwindling revenues.

Though they approach the issue with the best of intentions, the results are often less than what they hoped for. Those who are the quickest to throw their hands in the air have often convinced themselves that poor alignment is an immutable fact of life. Even those who have decided that concerted action is necessary to tackle collaborative issues inside their organizations are skeptical when they are told – as I often tell them – that collaborative issues are solvable.

There is a tested and proven method to produce the kind of collaboration that today's organizations need to thrive. What could a dramatic improvement in team morale mean for your business? What difference could the following numbers make for you and for your organization?

✓ **Up to 27% more sales revenue**

✓ **Up to 36% more gross profit**

✓ **Up to 42% higher sales lead conversion rate**

✓ **Up to 33% faster ramp-up time for new sales reps**

All just by Sales focusing on selling and Marketing focusing on supporting Sales through good marketing.

Crucially, the OneTEAM Method™ is not a shortcut, nor is it a quick fix 'Band-Aid' solution. It is a holistic solution.

The handful of disconnected metrics and processes that business consultants bring to bear on the issue of poor collaboration – well-intentioned though they may be – are not the panacaeae that they claim them to be. By the same token, techno-centric solutions that are peddled by technology vendors are proving, for many, to be costly snake oil. The reality is, if the human element isn't satisfactorily addressed then all the metrics and technology in the world won't help remedy the situation.

In the end, the problem's thickest root is the people within the organization. The communication problems that need to be solved begin and end with them.

Technology, processes and metrics will not solve the issue on their own, but they will help maintain the virtuous cycle of collaboration that results only once the communication problems between Sales and Marketing have been addressed once and for all.

To call a strategy "holistic" – as I have done – it must take into account the three intermeshing gears of viable and sustainable Sales+Marketing Collaboration. The OneTEAM Method™ addresses all of the elements within an organization: the People, the Processes, and the Technology (the descending order of priority for these three elements, as we shall see later in the book, is of utmost importance).

I call this the Productivity Trinity, and it is the foundation upon which

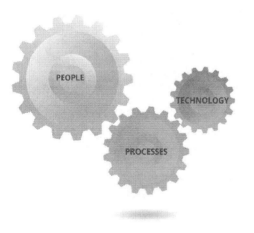

successful implementation of the OneTEAM Method™ is built.

We will hear more about the Productivity Trinity later.

Although I developed the OneTEAM Method in Australia, it is, in fact, readily applicable almost everywhere in the world. The strategies that I will outline in this book recognize no borders. The online world has, few would dispute, long ago made borders a dispensable concept. So, rest assured, no matter where in the world you are reading this book, you too can use the OneTEAM Method™ to build and maintain a collaborative cycle in your organization (and to reap the substantial benefits as well).

Chapter Takeaway

The OneTEAM Method™ is the holistic answer to the problem at the root of poor Sales+Marketing Collaboration. It is applicable and available worldwide, and its tested and proven steps can dramatically improve the state of collaboration within your organization. We will return to the Method later, but for now I want to turn to the difference between mere alignment and true collaboration.

Peter Strohkorb

Chapter 3:
More than just Team Alignment, Collaboration is the Key

In my almost twenty years of working in both executive sales and strategic marketing roles for some of the world's largest corporations, I have personally witnessed the degree to which waste and frustration abound when Sales and Marketing collaborate poorly or not at all. Unfortunately, this is an all-too-common phenomenon in both B2B and B2C businesses all over the world. My experience has taught me time and again that waste (of time, money and resources), frustration, and the issues that inevitably follow in the wake of each are not only manageable, they are thoroughly avoidable.

Fortunately, the success that so many collaborative organizations are enjoying is repeatable. Just imagine for a moment what a synergistic Sales/Marketing partnership could do for your organization. Imagine an organization in which there is a symbiotic relationship between Sales and Marketing; an organization in which each department knows exactly what the other needs to be successful; an organization in which proactive inter-departmental communication hones content to a fine point and makes the most from sales leads; an organization that shares and responds to customer feedback and market insight on a macro level. Such an organization, no matter what its products or services, would be either an industry leader or well on its way to becoming one. Such an organization would enjoy the envy of its peers, the trust of its clients and the support of its owners and shareholders.

At every turn, our research and my experience have led me to the same conclusion: The way to make both departments stronger is to establish – as early as possible – a healthy collaborative relationship between Sales and Marketing. Cooperation – especially when it is effectively managed – can increase revenues, profits and customer satisfaction levels. Importantly, a collaborative corporate culture also makes an organization more attractive to quality workforce candidates; it can boost morale and make it easier to recruit and retain valuable staff. Collaborative enterprizes are not only more successful; they are magnetic: they pull quality customers and staff into their orbit and keep them there.

Some Sources of Collaborative Friction

The Internet is full of stories about poor Sales+Marketing Collaboration. In my LinkedIn Group, the Sales+Marketing Collaboration Community, much of the conversation focuses on the disconnect between Sales and Marketing and its various manifestations, which run the gamut all the way from the amusing to the infuriating.

In conversations with leading executives, I have also found almost universal agreement: Sales and Marketing don't work together as well as they should.

Are we targeting the customer, or each other ?

While there is not complete agreement as to the causes of collaborative friction, there are three issues that consistently rise to the surface. Here they are, in no particular order:

Accountability Differences

It is very easy to measure sales performance: either reps hit their sales target or they don't. This is not the case with Marketing. They concern themselves with promotions, campaigns, brand recognition, business profile, lead generation, and other 'soft' objectives. It is, therefore, more difficult to measure Marketing and to make it accountable than it is to do the same for Sales.

By the same token, it is easier to frame Marketing as a cost center with perhaps questionable or even negligible value. It is an easy target for CEOs, i.e. in difficult times it is often the marketing budget that finds itself in the crosshairs. For this reason, too many marketers are living in almost constant fear for their job security. Marketing automation vendors often prey on these fears, claiming that their software will produce efficiencies and insightful data to justify the increased marketing budget. However, the increase in marketing technology spend only further exacerbates the situation if the technology implementation does not translate to immediate sales results (and, on its own, it very rarely does).

Personality Differences

It may be a bit of a cliché but, generally speaking, sales reps and marketing people are made out of different stuff. Sales reps are often more outgoing, more likely to embrace risk, and they are often more short-term-reward-oriented. Marketers on the other hand often tend to be more introverted than salespeople. They tend to think either in more artistic ways (think advertising) or more analytically (think data mining) than their Sales counterparts. They tend to focus further down the road – indeed, their strategies often depend on broader, more long-term thinking, and their thought processes are more often than not big-picture. As cliché (counterproductive even) as it may be to say so, there is a grain of truth in the old assertion that salespeople and marketers might as well be from different planets. Given these differences, it is little wonder that building a productive relationship between the two departments is easier said than done.

Educational Differences

Different levels and types of education remain some of the biggest roadblocks to effective Sales+Marketing Collaboration. In their less guarded moments, some marketers admit to feeling intellectually superior to salespeople because they have spent years studying in pursuit of a formal marketing qualification, while sales people can, by and large, not make the same claim.

Why not? Because universities are not – not as yet at least – offering degrees in Sales. Instead, reps have to rely on vocational sales training courses and often on their own trial-and-error experience. This is not taking anything away from salespeople; they often have formal qualifications in other fields of study. In fact, some of the best salespeople I know have degrees in other disciplines, particularly in marketing. The best salespeople better understand the big picture by looking at it from both ends, namely from the marketing side as well as from the sales side. But such reps are rare beasts indeed and they are highly sought after, too.

This kind of educational imbalance can lead to some rather nasty exchanges between Sales and Marketing. I have seen some marketers represent salespeople as uneducated troglodytes or knuckle-draggers. I have seen salespeople return fire, claiming that marketers are bottle-fed ivory tower types without the slightest understanding of the real world. Although separate knowledge- and skill-development paths are often a source of friction between sales and marketing people, they don't have to be. The friction is rarely itself caused by these educational differences; rather, it is the symptom of a larger underlying problem. Some people initially are tempted to use these differences as a kind of cheap shot to make a quick point, but it seems to me that over time this can lead to more entrenched attitudes and beliefs that are not at all conducive to quality team collaboration. Consequently, I have found that addressing the larger, underlying issues leads to a rapid evaporation of the conflicts that seem to revolve around educational disparities.

There are many more organizationally specific issues that I have encountered, but the three points above are the ones that seem to continually resurface in my conversations with sales and marketing executives. This book is a product of the frustration that I encountered – and felt – surrounding this admittedly well-travelled ground. Rather than more discussion of the differences between salespeople and marketers, it is time to forge a new path forward, one that helps both salespeople and marketers realize their full potential without getting hung up on the differences between the two functions and their representatives.

Collaboration: The Key to Improving the Customer Experience

The digital economy and the Buyer's Journey have revolutionized the way that people and organizations buy, particularly when it comes to large B2B sales. While it was once enough to have a relationship with one's customers to secure their loyalty, it has become increasingly apparent that, especially in competition-saturated vertical markets, the *quality* of these relationships is a driving factor in attracting, satisfying and retaining customers.

Sales and Marketing are, of course, two of the most customer-facing functions in any organization. They may not be the face of the organization in the boardroom, but they certainly are that face in the marketplace. Customers gauge organizations by the way sales and marketing departments speak to and with them. Since today's buyers report that they are looking for quality and consistency in this dialogue, you would think that the senior management team's top priority would be to ensure that these two vital functions perform in perfect harmony so that they best represent the organization to customers and prospects.

With surprising frequency this is not the case. Yet, Sales+Marketing Collaboration is the ideal vehicle to align customer-facing business processes and messaging in order to enhance the customer experience all along the Buyer's Journey. It can become a strategic advantage.

Therefore, symbiotic Sales+Marketing Collaboration needs to become more than a 'would be nice to have': It needs to become a top priority for organizations of all shapes and sizes everywhere. If your organization is not either overhauling or fine-tuning this important relationship right now, you can be sure that your competitors are.

To understand an organization's collaboration stats quo the OneTEAM Method™ proposes that there is a collaboration maturity spectrum, i.e. that there are different collaborative stages through which an organization can grow or mature.

The lowest maturity stage is characterized by what I call the 'Silo Mindset'. Here, the two corporate departments (un)happily co-exist, often without much interaction but lots of prejudice. This is the typical scenario where Marketing throws sales leads and collateral over the fence to Sales and wipes its hands of any downstream consequences. "We've done our work," they say, "now it's up to Sales to sell." Sales looks at the leads and says,

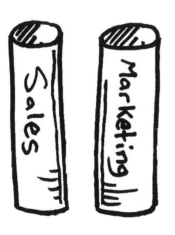

"These are no good," promptly and permanently ignoring them. The same process is repeated with marketing collateral.

Sales hastily concludes that Marketing lives in its own world, that it doesn't support Sales, nor understand its needs. Marketing jumps to its own conclusions, usually pertaining to Sales' supposed inability to sell anything at all. This kind of cycle, if left unchecked, has not – at least not to my knowledge – ever resolved itself.

The next maturity stage through which would-be collaborative organizations must pass is what I call the 'Process Mindset'. At this point, the two departments have realized that they are better off working together in some, albeit limited, way.

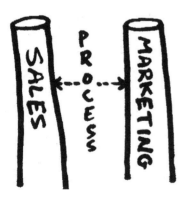

Process Mindset collaboration is limited to a small number of narrowly defined processes, the most popular one being the generation, nurturing and handover of sales leads. This is also one of the popular 'quick-fix solutions' that management likes to throw at the problem of poor Sales+Marketing Collaboration. More on that later.

Less mature organizations treat sales lead management as a one-way process as described above, whereas in the more mature organizations this process is much more bi-directional, with information flowing back to Marketing from Sales in terms of lead follow up and closure rates.

But even this is less than ideal.

The really mature organizations have discovered that there is much more to marketing than the generation of sales leads and marketing content. These mature organizations understand the importance of a united front; from the customers' perspective, Sales and Marketing have become nearly indistinguishable from each other. They have developed what I call the 'Collaboration Mindset'. Such a mindset – to

deserve the name – must be pervasive. Most importantly, it must unfailingly deliver the kind of personalized and nuanced customer experience that organizations have been talking about for years, but rarely have delivered. Such organizations live and breathe the term 'Smarketing'.

It is difficult to overstate the importance of effective Sales+Marketing Collaboration for organizations that want to address the needs and expectations of today's customers.

Think of Sales and Marketing as the two legs of a long-distance runner. Since the customer is only interested in the leaders of the pack and misalignment between sales and marketing functions significantly impedes organizational foot speed, it is crucial that organizations not fall behind. Hobbled or (at the very least) limping organizations are rapidly doing so, lagging behind twenty-first-century buying trends. More than ever they need to have both legs pumping in unison for maximum efficiency. They need to use their energy to propel the organizational body so that it can out-sprint the competition in the era of the digital economy and the Buyer's Journey.

Chapter Takeaway

We touched on the significance of positive customer experience and how consistent messaging from both Sales and Marketing is essential to building customer confidence and trust. And we looked at different mindsets across the collaboration maturity spectrum and the significance of creating a consistent customer experience, which should propel foot-dragging organizations into the kind of processes necessary to forge a better Sales/Marketing relationship.

Chapter 4:
The Numbers Don't Lie

There is a mountain of evidence that supports this book's premise, namely that Sales+Marketing Collaboration is good for business and that its opposite, isolation leads to misalignment and to undesirable business outcomes. Researchers from around the world have quantified these negative business outcomes, so here is a small selection of their findings:

Forrester's 2011 research report, "B2B Sales and Marketing Alignment Starts with the Customer," confirms the dysfunctional and damaging gap that still exists between Sales and Marketing in the vast majority of B2B organizations. They found that:

- Fewer than 1 in 10 of the B2B organizations surveyed claimed to have tight alignment between their Sales and Marketing functions

- Nearly 7 out of 10 evaluated their performance as average or below average

*https://www.forrester.com/B2B+Sales+And+Marketing+Alignment+Starts+With+The+Customer/fulltext/-/E-RES58165

According to Marketing Profs*, the TAS Group, in a study in conjunction with Salesforce.com, found that "over 67% of Sales professionals do not achieve their personal sales quota". However, they also found that in organizations with good Sales and Marketing alignment "revenue achievement is as much as 25% higher," that "high performers are 57% more likely to work there," and that these aligned organizations enjoy "a 15% higher win rate".

* http://www.marketingprofs.com/chirp/2013/11909/10-things-every-sales-manager-should-know-about-sales-performance-infographic

The **Aberdeen Group** (# http://www.aberdeen.com/research/8669/ra-sales-marketing-alignment/content.aspx) reported in 2011 in their market research report that: *"Highly aligned organizations achieve an average of 32% annual revenue growth."*

They followed this up with a more extensive 2013 study, in which they found that aligned organizations were well ahead of the performance curve:

- 84% of sales reps achieved quota vs. a 55% industry average

- 13.7% average year-on-year increase in average deal size or contract value vs. a 3.4% industry average

- 10.9% average year-on-year increase in overall sales team attainment of sales quota vs. a 1.1% industry average increase

A 2013 study by MathMarketing (http://www.mathmarketing.com/) found that:

- Joint planning between Sales and Marketing teams can lead, on average, to 62% more revenue

Their research also showed that aligned organizations:

- Grow 5.4% faster year-on-year than their competitors

- Are 38% better at closing proposals than non-aligned businesses

- Churn 36% fewer of their customers than their competitors each year

Sirius Decisions (http://www.siriusdecisions.com/blog/?s=B2B+sales+and+marketing) found that:

- B2B organizations with tightly aligned sales and marketing operations achieved 24% faster three-year revenue growth and 27% faster three-year profit growth

Sales Benchmark Index (SBI) (http://www.salesbenchmarkindex.com/) reports that:

- Up to 60% of sales leads are stuck at 'Do Nothing' or 'Wait and See'

- When Sales and Marketing are aligned, lead conversion (closed deals) rates are 2-3 times higher

According to a recent Optimizo (http://optimizosolutions.com/benchmarking/) report Forrester says: *"67% of CEOs now consider Marketing and Sales alignment as a top priority."*

Finally, also as reported by Optimizo, in a study that included more than 1,150 companies, the **MHI Institute** found that alignment was helping collaborative organizations close 67% more deals. Additionally, they found that those operating at the highest levels were, by and large, also the most collaborative.

Their findings are summarized below:

Business Issues*	World-Class Sales Organizations	All Respondents (n=1155)
Collaboration across departments when pursuing large deals	94%	43%
Understanding customer issues before proposing a solution	93%	48%
Alignment between Sales and Marketing in what customers want and need	91%	38%
Getting comparable value in return when giving price concessions	71%	21%
Leveraging the best practices of top performers to improve everybody else	89%	29%
A CRM system that is highly effective in enabling the organization to collaborate across departments	61%	23%

My own research confirms the accuracy of the findings that I have highlighted above. In a 2013/14 study (http://www.ps-consulting.com.au/market-research-findings.php) that included 185 B2B organizations, I reported a direct and undeniable link between high levels of Sales+Marketing Collaboration and financial business success.

The graph here illustrates this point from the opposite perspective: Organizations with poor Sales+Marketing Collaboration are twice as likely to suffer financially. Not 10% or 20%, they are *twice as likely* to suffer loss !

"Organizations with low Sales+Marketing Collaboration almost double the risk of experiencing declining sales."

How low Sales+Marketing Collaboration relates to declining sales

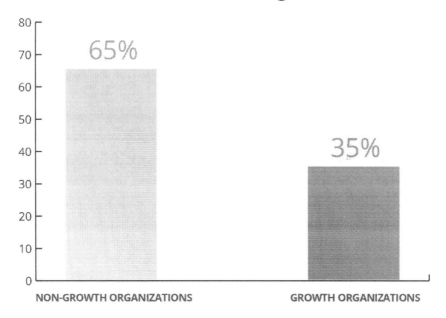

It is clear that Sales and Marketing misalignment is not a remotely acceptable situation for organizations with an eye on the future. Make no mistake: functional and effective communication between Sales and Marketing can be the difference between massive success and dismal failure.

As we have seen above, increasing the effectiveness of communication between Sales and Marketing can make the difference between success and failure in today's business climate.

As we have long known, small but tangible changes can result in the kind of growth that can propel organizations to the next level.

Stephen Hindman and John Sviokla's oft-cited table) from their 1992 Harvard Business School paper show how just a 5% increase in sales effectiveness can increase profits by a massive 20%.

(http://books.google.hu/books?id=a75y8uha0BwC&pg=PA198&lpg=PA198&dq=hindman+sviokla&source=bl&ots=XcHxPo8VR3&sig=3FpXk1AYTT8oMu-WA5GsMM7MPg&hl=en&sa=X&ei=LUZ7U5qSIciAyAOXmoDABQ&redir_esc=y#v=onepage&q=hindman%20sviokla&f=false)

They called it *"a four-fold profit multiplier"*.

To flesh out the significance of this phenomenon further, here is a generic but nonetheless compelling example of an organization with 40 sales reps and $100m in annual revenue. Let's not go crazy with the numbers, let's see what happens when we enable the sales force to win just 5% more sales deals, or if we supported them to free up just 5% of their 'stuck' deals.

5% Higher Sales Productivity	Baseline	Year 1	Year 2	Year 3	TOTALS
Annual Sales Target (assume 0% annual growth)	$100,000,000	$100,000,000	$100,000,000	$100,000,000	
Number of Sales People	100	100	100	100	
Total Actual Sales	$100,000,000	$105,000,000	$110,250,000	$115,762,500	
Incremental Revenue Increases		$5,000,000	$5,250,000	$5,512,500	$15,762,500
Profit Margin (Assume constant)	30%	30%	30%	30%	
Incremental Profit Gain		$1,500,000	$1,575,000	$1,653,750	$4,728,750

As you can see, even just a 5% increase in sales productivity represents an enormous benefit to both the business as a whole and to the individual reps' commissions.

Everybody wins in a collaborative organization.

Unfortunately for those who continue to drag their heels, the inverse is also true: sales productivity suffers when there is a lack of cooperation between Sales and Marketing. Turn the above formula on its head so that the organization loses 5% more deals, or that 5% more deals become stuck. Feed a negative number into Hindman and Sviokla's formula and the results are equally staggering, but not in a good way:

5% Lower Sales Productivity	Baseline	Year 1	Year 2	Year 3	TOTALS
Annual Sales Target (assume 0% annual growth)	$100,000,000	$100,000,000	$100,000,000	$100,000,000	
Number of Sales People	100	100	100	100	
Total Actual Sales	$100,000,000	$95,000,000	$90,250,000	$85,737,500	
Incremental Revenue Increases		$(5,000,000)	$(4,750,000)	$(4,512,500)	$(14,262,500)
Profit Margin (Assume constant)	30%	30%	30%	30%	
Incremental Profit Gain		$(1,500,000)	$(1,425,000)	$(1,353,750)	$(4,278,750)

As you can see, even just a very small decrease in sales won can have a devastating impact on any business, where it stands in relation to its competitors, and the fortunes of its employees (all of them, not just salespeople and marketers, but particularly those whose compensation is related to revenues).

We will take a more detailed look at the financial benefits of the OneTEAM Method™ in Chapter 15.

Chapter Takeaway

All the research paints the same picture and leads us to the same inevitable conclusion: Heel-dragging organizations ignore collaborative issues at tremendous risk to their sales performance, which is the foremost indicator of their ability to survive in the twenty-first-century marketplace. Successful organizations are those that have been most willing to adopt the new model and adapt to changing market conditions.

Doing nothing is not an option.

Peter Strohkorb

Chapter 5:
Growing Pains

What has struck me over the years is that the larger the organization, the more likely it is to suffer from collaborative issues. In fact, at least in terms of collaborative potential, smaller – and therefore more flexible – organizations actually seem to have a significant competitive advantage over larger ones. As organizations take on more staff and extend their reach into new territories, collaboration issues often grow apace with this expansion, usually manifesting in an entrenched 'us vs. them' attitude between Sales and Marketing.

There is an academic explanation for this phenomenon. In the late '70s, Massachusetts Institute of Technology Professor Thomas J. Allen researched the frequency of interactions between professional services people (in this case engineers), comparing the frequency of interactions with the literal distance between them.

Famously, the research showed that the frequency of communication decreased exponentially with the distance. This quickly came to be known as the Allen Curve, a visualization of which you can see here.

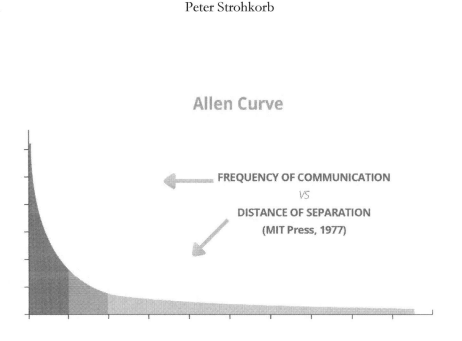

Allen Curve

FREQUENCY OF COMMUNICATION
vs
DISTANCE OF SEPARATION
(MIT Press, 1977)

Later, with advancements in telecommunications technology, and then again with the advent of social media, the validity of the Allen Curve was challenged. Critics claimed that the Allen Curve may once have been accurate for physical separation but that the increasingly digital world had rendered it obsolete.

However, using the example of telephony, Allen questioned the seemingly common-sensical notion that, as connective technology advances, so too does the level of connectivity between individuals in geographically distinct locations.

It boils down to this: by and large, people communicate most readily with those in their immediate physical environment; technology has less impact on this than one might assume. Face-to-face communication and physical proximity are, as my own experience and research have also shown, important drivers of communication, collaboration and productivity.

As businesses grow, is it inevitable that they develop collaborative problems apace with their growth? Not necessarily.

The OneTEAM Method™ does more than remedy an existing Sales+Marketing Collaboration deficiency. In fact, it can also be applied to prevent the collaboration issues that come from poor or insufficient communication from arising in the first place.

Many of the organizations I have helped have experienced these growing pains and their related collaborative issues first hand. Pro-actively applying the OneTEAM Method™ gives growing businesses the tools that they need to address the un-cooperative mindsets and practices that are causing these pains. While stretching at the seams is to be expected as organizations grow, the right strategies can help businesses to accommodate this growth, and future growth as well.

Once organizations grow to a certain size – usually when their sales and marketing teams stop sharing the same physical space and/or the same supporting staff – maintaining constructive dialogue between Sales and Marketing becomes an increasingly difficult job. As they drift apart physically, a mental distance between departments begins to form as well. Attitudes, perceptions, and priorities may intersect, but they are rarely aligned. Each department has, it seems, its own agenda. Mutual respect and trust may become all but completely absent.

In smaller organizations, sales and marketing departments often share a physical space, a physical proximity that facilitates, if not collaboration, then at least frequent communication. Even if inter-department collaboration is not a part of the organization's business strategy, results can resemble those of collaboratively structured organizations simply because the two departments are living cheek by jowl. They can simply overhear each other, lean over to the next cubicle and ask a quick question or call a short impromptu meeting. In other words they are problem solving together. Not only are they on the same floor, they're on the same page.

For many of these smaller organizations, a strong matriarch or patriarch is the glue that binds the organization together. There is a collective loyalty that flows in both directions, and purpose and vision alignment usually means that everybody is pulling in the same direction.

Contrast this with organizations that have left these early stages far behind them. The CEO of these large organizations is the head of a wide range of functional silos, each with their own executive leader who in turn reports to the CEO or to the COO. Sales and Marketing are now only a piece of a bigger puzzle that may include Manufacturing, Administration and Finances, Research and Development, HR, Procurement, Legal, Warehousing, et al. Often finding themselves in a sea of data, CEOs rarely have the bandwidth to delve into the minutiae of each reporting line, so they delegate these responsibilities to their dedicated executive department heads.

Most often, it is when an organization transitions into this stage that Sales and Marketing are split into two separate departments, each with their own executive heads and with separate reporting lines. What this means is that there is a – perhaps inadvertent – top-down preparedness to keep sales and marketing departments in their separate silos. The heads of sales departments are generally tasked with growing sales revenue, protecting sales margins, and representing the organization in its engagement with customers.

The heads of Marketing are often concerned with brand profile, market share, and corporate image. Each is given metrics in the form of role-specific key performance indicators (KPIs), which measure performance according to agreed-upon parameters (usually those listed above). Budgets, remuneration and bonuses are then based upon performance according to these narrow metrics.

Since these metrics rarely intersect, Sales and Marketing often end up working in their own worlds, with little to no understanding of each other's roles within the organization. Each department prioritizes and objectivizes differently, and they begin the process of almost inevitable cultural drift that leads to inter-departmental rifts, and in some cases that I have seen, even to out-and-out hostility. They begin to develop niche skills and languages; they promote and hire staff according to increasingly narrow criteria, and they dig in.

While this may not be true in every organization, small differences, if allowed to fester, can become barbed-wire fences between Sales and Marketing over time. Marketing ends up merely throwing sales leads over the fence to Sales, wiping their hands and saying, "That's our job done. Now it's up to Sales to sell."

When Salespeople, picking up these leads, find themselves unable to convert them into sales they throw them back over the fence, or worse, reject them out of hand and begin to ignore them altogether. Each side then accuses the other of incompetence: Marketing claims that Sales can't sell, and Sales says that Marketing does not know how to support them.

So how do large or growing organizations prevent these kinds of disputes from arising, or, if they have already emerged, what can be done to reverse the trend?

As with every journey, the first step is the most important one. The first step, as we shall see, is recognizing that you have a collaboration problem.

Chapter Takeaway

We explored how team collaboration tends to diminish with distance, regardless of whether it is physical, mental or even attitudinal distance. Bringing teams back together (if possible through closer physical proximity) is an important part of collaborative success.

Peter Strohkorb

Chapter 6:
Insights from the World of
Psychology

Some authors have tried to explain the often-poor communication between sales and marketing teams as one caused by personality differences. They argue that sales and marketing are not only career paths; they are, in and of themselves, personality types. A certain type of person, they say, is more naturally drawn towards the planning, strategizing, and concept-building that make up marketing work; sales work tends to draw a different kind of person – often those who relish the opportunity to exert their influence over others. I frequently encounter the metaphor of Martians and Venusians, which seems to make an appearance whenever the differences between salespeople and marketers are under discussion. No matter what metaphor we use to describe the two departments the frequent recourse to binary terms is, I think, an unhelpful oversimplification.

This doesn't mean I reject the personality hypothesis outrightly. Quite the contrary, when I began my research into Sales+Marketing Collaboration, I looked for evidence to shore up just such a personality divide, but I was frequently surprised (and occasionally frustrated) by the scarcity of material on the subject. What material there was seemed to be based, at best, on extremely small sample sizes or, at worst, on purely anecdotal evidence or utterly unfounded assumptions; the more I looked, the more convinced I became that the Martian/Venusian hypothesis is flawed.

In my search for a more plausible theory that accounted for the observed behavioral differences that separate salespeople and marketers, I came across a UK-headquartered psychological assessment group, Thomas International Ltd ((http://www.thomasinternational.net/en-au/ourassessments/PPA.aspx), that focuses much of their research on workplace dynamics. They assess more than 100,000 people each year in the UK, which gives them a great deal of data to work with. They have assessed almost 7,000 salespeople and almost 2,000 marketers in 2014 alone, and this has allowed them to paint a more nuanced picture of the behavioral preferences of each.

What makes their findings most interesting and plausible is the fact that they have not drawn a dividing line between Sales and Marketing and assigned those who work on one side of the fence to one categorical type, and those on the other side of the fence to the other. Their approach is more sophisticated. Their findings are based upon the Personal Profile Analysis (PPA), which presents participants with a list of four different adjectives. The PPA employs a forced-choice response method: the participant must choose two adjectives from each set of four (one that they feel describes them best and one that describes them the least). This is repeated 24 times with a different set of adjectives each time.

The results are then analyzed and respondents are presented with a profile which draws from elements of the following four categories: Dominance, Influence, Compliance and Steadiness (DISC).

We'll look at how frequently salespeople and marketers demonstrate the characteristics associated with these categories below, but first let's take a closer look at these four behavioural types and the characteristics that usually accompany them.

People who show a strong tendency toward DOMINANCE usually possess a number of the following characteristics:

- Assertive
- Competitive
- Direct
- Driving
- Forceful
- Inquisitive
- Self-starter

People who show a strong tendency toward INFLUENCE usually possess a number of the following characteristics:

- Communicative
- Friendly
- Influential
- Networker
- Persuasive
- Positive
- Verbal

People who show a strong tendency toward STEADINESS usually possess a number of the following characteristics:

- Amiable
- Deliberate
- Dependable
- Good listener
- Persistent
- Thorough

People who show a strong tendency toward COMPLIANCE usually possess a number of the following characteristics:

- Accurate
- Careful
- Compliant
- Logical
- Perfectionist
- Precise
- Systematic

Instead of thinking of each of these archetypes as a distinct territory with definite boundaries separating it from the others, Thomas International measures the tendency that each individual has toward each of the archetypes. A high score in terms of both Dominance and Steadiness reveals a behavioral type that is made up of a blend of the two characteristics. The test reveals tendencies without pigeonholing respondents, and it is for this reason that it is extremely useful when we use it to understand the potential behavioral conflicts between Sales and Marketing.

As you can see in the graphic I've provided here, there is a significant degree of similarity in the behavioral characteristics of salespeople and marketers. They are, for instance, both highly inclined toward Influence, meaning that both tend toward the impulsive and (perhaps surprisingly) the cooperative. This helps us to locate at least part of the source of their conflict: both sides may try to persuade one another to their point of view, determined to have the last word. At the same time, it shows that there is a great deal of potential for cooperative enterprize, provided that neither side feels it is being forced into an unfair compromise. This is also the key to effective collaboration.

So much for the similarities. In all the other categories, there are significant differences. Salespeople are far more inclined to Dominance, and marketers tend to drift more toward Compliance. The most observable difference between Dominance and Compliance is that Dominant individuals are big-picture thinkers; they're enterprising and play the long game with little desire to get caught up in details. In contrast, Compliant individuals typically possess a perfectionist streak, focus on details and employ a systematic approach to their work. These two pieces of the puzzle fit nicely into each other. While it doesn't mean (not by a long shot) that all salespeople domineer over their less assertive marketing counterparts, it does show how a slight imbalance in the two tendencies can, over time, create an uneven power relationship.

Marketers also tend more toward Steadiness than salespeople. This, like the unequal power dynamic in the example above, might contribute to the continuation of a less-than-ideal situation in the name of not rocking the boat. Like the other tendencies here, it is important to recognize that these are not hard and fast categories, but these differences, even if they are slight, and their implications are highly instructive for someone, like myself, who is interested in creating a more harmonious relationship between Sales and Marketing.

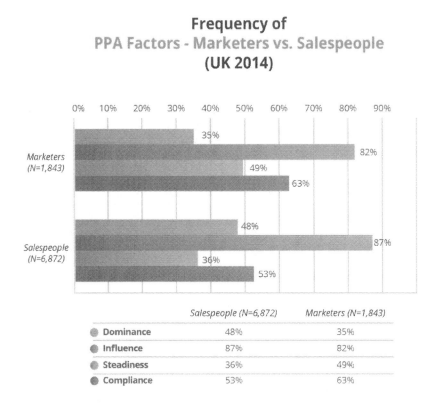

Frequency of
PPA Factors - Marketers vs. Salespeople
(UK 2014)

	Salespeople (N=6,872)	Marketers (N=1,843)
● Dominance	48%	35%
● Influence	87%	82%
● Steadiness	36%	49%
● Compliance	53%	63%

Language Barriers

I'd like to add something to the conversation, something that I have noticed in my own research and in my work with organizations that find themselves in the midst of collaborative difficulties. The lack of cooperation between salespeople and marketers may or may not be related to the way they are wired, but I think there might be something of a linguistic issue at play as well. The two departments, as they each have grown increasingly specialized, have drifted apart in terms of the language(s) they speak. Inside departments, everybody may be using the same phrasebook, but when the two departments come together, they have difficulty understanding, and being understood, by the other.

Even if both sides do understand the lingua franca of revenue, the distinctly different languages of Marketing and Sales rely upon very different grammars: they take different things for granted, speak from different perspectives, yet each with their own trusted authorities. They speak over each other's heads, and their respective terms of reference are often miles apart. Sales usually addresses customers in a way that leans towards individual and often more near-term needs. Marketing on the other hand addresses the needs of the market in more abstract, longer-term and more broadly inclusive ways.

If we are going to move forward in a way that is truly collaborative, we need to address the proven personality differences between salespeople and marketers, but we also need to make sure that, when they come to the table, they're speaking a language that makes sense to each of them.

The languages of Sales and Marketing may well remain distinct for each department, but when they do come together for a common cause, there needs to be either a common language or at least a competent translator between them. The other key prerequisite is that there is an open feedback loop not only from Marketing to Sales but also one going back the other way. We need to close this loop in order to open up communications in a constructive and continuous fashion. We'll talk about closing this loop in more detail later on.

Chapter Takeaway

The only reliable way to effect a results-based dialogue between Sales and Marketing is to make sure that there is an agreed-upon language – or at the very least a translator – in place between them. Finding common ground (language and otherwise) needs to begin as early in the relationship-building stages as possible.

Chapter 7:
Some Common Symptoms of
Sales/Marketing Misalignment

As I have already shown, misalignment between Sales and Marketing is a very real problem – one that can seriously impede organizations in their attempt to keep pace with today's customers and their expectations. The problem is too large to ignore, but still, some of the symptoms of poor collaboration might go unnoticed, even if you're looking for them. If we don't know exactly what it is that we're looking for, it's unlikely that we'll ever find it.

In this chapter we will take a detailed look at some of the symptoms of Sales/Marketing misalignment (some obvious, some less so) and investigate their potential causes.

In no particular order, they are as follows:

1. Symptom: Sales revenue numbers are disappointing

This may sound like an overly broad and perhaps even an obvious statement, but it is nevertheless true that the goal of nearly every business is to experience year-on-year growth. This exerts a constantly building pressure on the sales force, which is expected to grow sales revenue and margins continuously. This pressure often builds to intolerable levels in poorly aligned organizations, coming to a head when sales revenue contracts or remains stagnant for long enough to raise the eyebrows (or voices) of senior executives. By the time this point has been reached, the problem has almost always put down roots so deep and tangled as to make the issue seem insurmountable.

It is no surprise, therefore, that whether I am sought out as a first or a last resort by organizations that are experiencing collaborative issues, disappointing sales results rank very high (often #1 with a bullet) on the list of grievances that organizations cite when they bring me in to address an issue.

Since it is highly risky to wait until an organization is plagued with deeply entrenched attitudes and barricaded communication channels, early intervention – or, even better, proactive prevention – is the key to success.

Smart and successful companies are those that pull success-impeding weeds out of their soil by the roots well before they have the opportunity to grow so large as to become unmanageable. Smarter and more successful still are the ones that apply a weed-preventing and eradicating agent early on, well before they even have a chance to sprout.

That said, there's no reason to jump to conclusions. Misalignment is not the only reason for low sales numbers. You might have an under-motivated or even a low-quality sales force, an ill-conceived marketing strategy, an inefficient sales funnel, a lag in sales due to long ramp-up times for newly hired salespeople, poor hiring processes, too much discounting by the sales force, an inferior product/service, poor leadership, or even a toxic business culture. Whatever it is, there are organizations just like yours that have recognized and addressed these same issues, and there are scores of tools and strategies that have proven to be effective in terms of improving sales closing ratios and lifting revenue.

However, it seems that many organizations have grown obsessed with these quick-fix, Band-Aid solutions, which bring tight focus to discrete issues while ignoring the larger underlying issues that have allowed them to become problematic in the first place. Sales training and automation systems can absolutely help, as long as the issue is not the symptom of a larger problem. A vast array of problems can be traced back to poor inter-personal and inter-departmental communication and collaboration, so before you shell out for these 'point' solutions, first make sure that collaborative issues aren't at the root of your issues.

This demands no small amount of big-picture thinking. It is often hard to see the bigger picture when you are yourself inside of the frame. Sometimes it really pays to have an independent set of eyes take a fresh and unencumbered look at the business.

This objectivity is absolutely crucial if you want to grasp the sales revenue problem at the root and eradicate it with a firm yank, once and for all.

2. Symptom: Blame and frustrations abound

Inter-departmental finger pointing and antagonisms are where poor communication between departments most often comes to a head. Inter-departmental friction is most commonplace in the organizations in which Sales and Marketing operate in their own discrete operational silos.

When times are good Sales may well puff up its own chest, claiming skill and technique make all the difference, while Marketing may say that behind strong organizational performance is its brand building, market positioning, promotional campaigns and high quality sales collateral, leads and content.

While times are good, these disputes are, for the most part, relatively good-natured and seemingly harmless. However, when revenue begins to fall out of alignment with sales quotas and the pressure cooker of expectations begins to be felt in both departments then inter-departmental antagonism can quickly go from latent to blatant. Since Sales is immersed in a feedback loop that includes immediate and direct interactions with customers, Marketing often gains its feedback via very different mechanisms, such as market surveys, focus groups, or information bought from market intelligence firms. Thus, when Sales and Marketing come together under these circumstances, particularly when they are already pre-armed with grievances or disappointments, their disputes can get out of hand quickly.

Sales may start to complain about Marketing's poor quality collateral. Marketing may counter-punch, alleging that the sales team is ineffective or even incompetent. Rather than productive communication, the overwhelming tone becomes one vacillating between defensiveness and antagonism. As not wanting to be held to account for weakening sales results is entirely natural, the blame game begins to overwhelm inter-departmental communications. The ensuing 'us vs. them' mentality may then color almost all of the interactions between the sales and marketing departments, and the workplace can become one characterized by rivalry and mistrust.

At this point, the Human Resources (HR) team is usually called in to address this cultural toxicity. In my experience, it is at this point that Band-Aid solutions like team-building exercises and offsite retreats start being floated as possible remedies. Since these solutions rarely address the underlying issue (namely, the ability of each department to communicate effectively with the other), the desired outcomes, if they appear at all, are often short lived.

In Chapter 12, I will describe a hypothetical organization, Silo Inc., that is characterized by the kind of poor communication and its resultant un-collaborative environment of mistrust and antagonism that I have so often seen first-hand, even in well-known multinational enterprizes. I can tell you from experience that these are not pleasant places to work. I've seen high-performing staff members escape (often with a sigh of relief) from such a toxic environment, taking their talents to other, often competing, organizations that feature a more collaboratively minded corporate culture.

Miscommunication and mistrust can significantly impact an organization's reputation, and always for the worse. As if struggling to attract and retain quality staff isn't bad enough, poorly aligned sales and marketing departments also affect the way that customers view the organization.

The illustration shows how messaging from Sales (engagement) and from Marketing (insight) can be affected when there is a lack of communication between departments. Since Sales and Marketing are two of the organization's main customer-facing functions, poorly aligned sales and marketing personnel translates to unacceptable levels of risk to an organization's ability to stay on message in all its customer interactions.

Even subtle differences in message can look to the market like confusion or dissimilation. This can lead to a reputation for ineptitude or a loss of the brand trust that is so important for today's customers, B2B and B2C alike. In this digital age, a poor reputation can become viral in no time, and nobody wants to work for or do business with an organization that has a bad name with its peers or, even worse, with its customers.

3. Symptom: Sales reps aren't focusing on selling

How much marketing-generated collateral is Sales utilizing? Less than you might think. Thanks in no small part to a dysfunctional relationship between Sales and Marketing, organizations seem to be tolerating an unacceptably large amount of marketing collateral and sales leads going to waste. IDC says, "Only 25% of sales leads and marketing collateral that Marketing creates is ever used by sales teams."

"Only 25% of sales leads and collateral that Marketing creates is ever used by sales teams". IDC

Organizations are virtually flushing a good part of their marketing spend down the drain. This problem is exacerbated when sales reps spend their precious time – the very time that they should be spending on selling – producing their own (often inconsistent) marketing content.

Why would Sales reps do this?

Marketing, with its strategic objective of brand and thought leadership, may (with the best of intentions) create content and leads that it honestly believes are exactly what is required to support the sales force.

Yet Sales, with its decidedly more short-term focus, is looking for quicker solutions to help them meet their short-term sales targets. Eventually, sales reps feel they can no longer rely on support from Marketing. Their lack of faith in Marketing leads them to take matters into their own hands. After all, they often tend to believe that they have the more immediate contact with the market and that they (and only they) know what it really takes to solicit interest and gain traction with prospects. By trying to be all things to all people, though, salespeople tend to stretch themselves thin. In some extreme cases, they may even make statements and claims that their marketing team will not (indeed, can not) stand behind.

In poorly aligned organizations, Marketing creates collateral and, figuratively speaking, "throws it over the fence" to Sales, wipes its hands and declares: "That's our job done. Now it's up to Sales to sell." Thanks to modern technology and the temptation that it can offer to forego face-to-face interactions altogether, this entire exchange often takes place in the digital domain. Most organizations have a central IT network drive or a shared file folder that is accessible by sales as well as marketing teams. In many organizations that I have been involved with, these shared file folders are referred to as "black holes". Everything that goes in is never to be seen again. Frequently, multiple versions of the same document exist across a maelstrom of files, often illogically sorted and frequently modified until they are utterly unintelligible, unmanaged and unmanageable. In short, they are of use to nobody.

Since salespeople often need to access on-point material in a hurry, it comes as no surprise that, as time passes, these black holes are used less and less by salespeople. Neglect begets yet more neglect, and these shared folders become little more than impenetrable time capsules containing nothing in any way relevant to ongoing business.

Nowhere is the language barrier between Sales and Marketing more apparent than in these shared repositories. When I have looked back at some of the documented sparring matches between Sales and Marketing that take place in or around these black holes, it is clear that neither side is able to make itself truly understood; the temptation to assume either an aggressive or a defensive postures (sometimes both at once) is, it seems, impossible to resist when other attempts to communicate have not had the intended results. What neither side seems to recognize is that without a common language and understanding, even well-intentioned attempts to communicate and come to an agreement surrounding marketing collateral often fall short of the mark. The resulting mess ultimately addresses the needs of neither department, and, when it is presented to prospects or clients or to the broader market, it does neither the organization nor its employees any favors.

It is baffling that marketing teams should spend good time, effort and resources creating sales collateral without knowing exactly how (or, indeed, whether) salespeople actually use this material. It's equally baffling that many sales professionals are going into sales meetings with their own self-made collateral. And yet, this is precisely what I am encountering in the field, particularly in large organizations that have Marketing and Sales working in separate areas, on different floors, in different buildings, states, or even in different countries (as is so often the case in multinational firms).

Whether they communicate face-to-face or digitally, Sales and Marketing need a new set of collaboration mechanisms that allow both departments to speak to each other in a mutually agreed-upon language. A language that allows for a constructive cycle of feedback, that moves in both directions and that allows each department to support the other like never before. Imagine the kind of results that organizations could see if Marketing and Sales were able to turn effective communication into concerted action. Marketing could better support Sales, and Sales could focus on what it does best: selling.

4. Symptom: Marketing is pandering to high-profile sales reps

High-performing salespeople are no shrinking violets; they have skin thick enough to cope with rejection on a regular basis without losing heart. Also, they are trained to be persuasive, so they are accustomed to getting their way. They often have concrete ideas about what will work for them in sales calls or presentations, and they don't like waiting, preferring to act decisively (not to say impulsively) rather than sit on their hands and wait for Marketing to deliver the content that they think they need.

I have seen particularly strong-willed sales reps storm into a marketing executive's office to tell them, in no uncertain terms, what they think of marketing-generated leads and collateral. They are not reluctant when it comes to offering their opinions, and they aren't shy about applying their often-considerable persuasive powers to get the kind of material they think they need to sell better.

Some of these salespeople seem to have more sway with Marketing than even senior executives. Marketing can find itself bending over backwards to please this extremely vocal minority, adopting collateral and even adjusting their strategy in a misguided attempt to appease a particularly insistent set of critics. Problems begin to mount when both this vocal minority and the marketing departments lose sight of the fact that not all salespeople – or, for that matter, customers – think alike. As long as a handful of vocal salespeople have a monopoly over what shape marketing collateral takes, marketing messages can become confused, costly market research can go under-utilized, and both departments can end up falling significantly short of what is expected of them. Nip this in the bud by putting tools and strategies in place that make sure communication is a dialogue, not a monologue.

5. Symptom: High-performing staff members are leaving

A staff turnover rate above the industry average is never a good sign. This becomes even more critical when an organization's top in-house talent is choosing to seek greener (usually more collaborative) pastures. A high turnover rate, especially when this includes an organization's top performers, can pull even large organizations into something of a death-spiral. A company that cannot retain its most talented people is rarely able to lure top performers away from their competition.

Finding, hiring and training replacements for your top performers who have left comes with a hefty price tag (usually tens of thousands of dollars) and significant delays (six months or more). Combining costs and delays like these can rapidly widen the gulf between the predicted and the actual sales figure. Such a discrepancy, especially if it is large enough to attract attention all the way up the chain, can have widespread negative consequences.

There are numerous factors that can contribute to a high staff turnover rate: poor management, toxic culture, less-than-desirable pay, unrealistic sales targets, and many others. In my conversations with some of the top salespeople and marketers and those who manage them, I have pinpointed a common cause: poor Sales+Marketing Collaboration. The atmosphere of hostility, the entrenched attitudes and the less-than-productive practices that typify misaligned organizations are positively repellent to top salespeople and marketers. Sales+Marketing Collaboration, whether poorly or perfectly executed, makes the decision easy for your top performers: We all love working in environments in which we feel both supported and supportive. Nobody wants to work in an organization in which effective communication and cooperation are impossible. Morale improves dramatically in a workplace that is made more supportive through collaboration, and that's not all:

Countless studies have shown that, as an organization's morale improves, so does its bottom line.

This is why those business environments that are structured and executed collaboratively tend to have turnover rates that are well below the industry average. You may have a handful of staff that you have nurtured straight out of university or elsewhere, but the chances are that the majority of your staff members have some experience of the working environment gained outside of your walls. If so, it is likely that they have experienced collaborative workplaces. In fact, the more familiar they are with the all-too-common 'us vs. them' environment and its inherent hostility, the more likely they are to pull up stakes before they become wrapped up in the drama.

Why devote so much of your time, energy and resources to training sales and marketing staff only to watch those with the highest potential move on to greener pastures? In doing so, they often take with them information that makes them all the more dangerous in terms of sharpening your competitors' teeth. What if, instead, you brought Sales and Marketing into accord, creating the kind of environment that not only retains high-performing staff but also draws top talent from other, less harmonious organizations?

A collaborative work environment can do more than increase revenue; it can dramatically affect the feelings of contentment and satisfaction within the organization. Such environments nurture existing talent and attract a whole new caliber of candidates.

6. Symptom: Change initiatives don't gain traction

So many of the organizations that come to me for help have, so they say, tried everything. They've tried marketing-centric organizational structures; they've tried sales-led approaches; they've reshuffled departments, created new positions and eliminated old ones; they've combined Sales and Marketing into a single department; they've split them into separate departments. And yet, no matter what the approach to the problem, the results remain less than satisfactory.

According to Patrick Spenner and Anna Bird of the Harvard Business Review in a paper, called "Marketers Flunk The Big Data Test" (https://hbr.org/2012/08/marketers-flunk-the-big-data-test), *"Half of [marketers'] information [comes] from their previous experience or their intuition about customers."* This is as much a problem as salespeople who are choosing to approach customers in their own way instead of using marketing-generated collateral.

Both stem from a degree of arrogance surrounding their own perception and knowledge of the customer's or the market's wants and needs. Marketing may rely on a variety of inputs, ranging from guide campaigns to online surveys, from gut instinct to, most recently, big data analytics and marketing automation, but salespeople tend to find this kind of data unconvincing.

The kind of data that marketers use can at times tell them things that are very unlike what salespeople are hearing directly from customers. Both sides are quite sure that they're right – and here's the kicker: both sides are right. But this doesn't help the tense relationship between Sales and Marketing. The fact that both sides are armed with evidence that supports their position makes it virtually certain that any approach that doesn't find common communicative ground is doomed to failure.

What is needed is an approach that addresses the ways in which Sales and Marketing engage with each other. This can only be achieved when there are effective collaborative structures in place that can make ongoing or future initiatives more successful. The inertia of 'doing nothing' or the passive, and at times subversive, resistance to change that often seems to plague larger organizations needs to be overcome as well, but the mere willingness to make changes – no matter on what scale – is often not enough. What is needed is a strategy that can turn the desire for a more productive and supportive workplace into a reality.

7. Symptom: Territorial disputes between Sales and Marketing

One of the largest barriers to effective collaboration between Sales and Marketing departments is the territorial disputes that so frequently occur in misaligned organizations. On one hand, there is the fencing off of discrete territories in which each department operates, independent from the other. With such an approach, lines in the sand are drawn, say, at the entrance to the funnel or pipeline, and so much as a toe across the line can make the offended parties begin to rattle their sabers. I have worked in such an environment, and I still clearly remember a number of times when individual-led attempts at innovation and initiative were briskly quashed with a stern look and words that should sound familiar to anybody who's worked in a misaligned organization: "That's not your job."

On the other hand, there is the opposite problem, namely that of an utter lack of boundaries between departments, which has similarly detrimental effects. Marketers effectively filling the shoes of salespeople (and vice versa) rarely translates to success. This is not to say that crossover should be avoided altogether. Rather, the overlapping areas between the two should be clearly assigned, understood and respected.

Some kind of boundary (albeit a semi-permeable one) should separate the two departments. I've never encountered a large and successful company that has managed to merge the two departments entirely into one. Organizations that do so are attempting to do too much in one step. They are trying to arrive at their destination without going through the necessary journey that precedes it and without grasping fully what their destination actually should be. Collaboration doesn't mean that boundaries disappear altogether. They merely blur, but not in ways that lead to the kind of territorial disputes that are so frequent in misaligned organizations.

The obstacle that needs to be overcome is the lack of formal understanding between Sales and Marketing as to how their responsibilities should, or should not, overlap. According to Amy Miller and Lisa Toner, 59% of marketers admit that there is no shared understanding between the two departments as to what the other's responsibilities are. Whether the boundary between departments is too porous or too impermeable, territorial disputes are inevitable when neither side knows precisely what the other should be doing, let alone what they are doing.

In later chapters I will lay out strategies for Marketing/Sales alignment procedures and strategies that have proven to help organizations not only avoid such needless territorial disputes but lift productivity and staff morale.

8. Symptom: Scarily low CRM adoption rates

According to CSO Insights, "CRM tool adoption rate is less than 50 percent" and "Fewer than 15 percent of organizations achieved improved win rates from implementing sales tools."

I have been part of enough CRM and other corporate technology implementations to notice a common pattern. The technology vendors display an attitude that seems to say, "Just put our technology in and everything will be fine."

However, it rarely is fine. Organizations leading with technology solutions that expect their people to become more productive overnight are kidding themselves. At one large multinational technology corporation that I worked with, the EVP of Sales and Marketing got up in front of the assembled crowd at the annual sales kick-off event and said these words in regards to the impending "go live" of the new CRM and ERP system: "We have planned everything to the nth degree. Nothing can go wrong."

If you think this sounds like the proverbial 'famous last words', you can probably guess what happened next. It was, from start to finish, an unmitigated disaster. So bad was it that a number of the parties even ended up dragging each other into court.

Several factors led to the high-profile failure of the project and to the ensuing sacking of the overconfident EVP I've quoted above. Here are some lessons that the organization unfortunately had to learn from experience:

- Do not expect project staff to work on the project while at the same time expecting them to fulfill their full-time day jobs effectively.

- Do not plan to turn off your legacy (current) system until the new system is working reliably, i.e. allow both the new and the old system to operate in parallel for a while.

- Do not rely on IT vendors and system integrators to act proactively in the best interest of the client or the end users.

- The business relationship has hit a low point when the parties feel they need to refer to the terms of the contract and get their lawyers involved.

- Don't just shove end users into a category that is flippantly dealt with under the heading "End User Training" (my personal favorite).

Why am I making this last point?

Because what happened was that all those people that had been happily using the old system and were very used to it were not really consulted when the new system was chosen and designed. They were merely expected to receive their end user training and start being productive on the new system almost instantly. Remember, in order to save cost and duplication of effort the old system was to be shut off at the same time as the new one went live. You can guess what happened next, can't you?

Despite their end user training the back end staff were expecting the new system to work similarly to the old one. After all, they had been expected to continue in their day job as well as absorb the intricacies of the new system. Most had taken an attitude of "I don't have time to learn the new system, I'll work it out when it goes live."

When it did, as you would expect, pretty much all the individual tasks ended up taking much longer than anyone expected, yet the tasks were expected to be completed just as quickly (if not faster) than with the old system. After all, the new system was meant to be more efficient than the old. The pressure mounted for the back end staff and for the management team and in the end the end users rebelled.

Let's just leave it here saying that the project ended up costing twice as much and taking about four times as long as was budgeted. Lawyers were called in, fingers were pointed and blame was attributed and rejected between the various parties involved. It was a disaster.

This incident does not seem to be an isolated one. Back in 2012, Accenture reported the following in "Connecting the Dots on Sales Performance": "The unvarnished truth is that a technology-centric approach has consistently failed to achieve results."

Like the Band-Aid solutions that I mentioned previously, blinkered focus on a particular problem often produces unsatisfactory and at times un-anticipated results. Automation can actually have negative revenue effects if the users are not educated in, and open to, the cooperative strategies that the technology enables. The same goes for processes, which are supported by the technology but remain practically useless employees commit to breaking bad habits and forming new and more productive ones.

Finally, the people within an organization can get the ball rolling in terms of collaboration (indeed, they are the most important factor in the collaborative equation), but they need the processes and technologies into which they can divert their energy. A shared, 'people-first' vision with agreed-upon objectives, processes and metrics will result in significantly higher technology adoption rates. People that take part in designing the solution will more readily accept that solution.

9. Symptom: New sales reps are taking too long to ramp up

According to the same Accenture 2012 report mentioned earlier, "Connecting the Dots on Sales Performance," "Almost 78% of newly hired sales reps take six months or longer to become fully proficient at selling."

The authors of the report also estimate that, during this ramp-up phase, each new rep costs the organization in excess of US$60,000, and this figure doesn't even include the time, effort and money invested during the often-lengthy and exhausting recruitment process!

The faster a new rep ramps up, the sooner the organization can see a return on both their pre- and post-hire investment. The inverse is also true: the longer reps take to ramp up, the longer it will be before the organization sees any kind of return on their investment. Multiply this effect by the number of new hires each year and it becomes utterly transparent that waiting longer than six months for reps to ramp up is not in any way acceptable.

Imagine how much better off an organization would be if its new sales reps were to ramp up faster. Even speeding up the onboarding process by as little as 10% can make a huge financial difference to both the employer and the employee.

How do we accelerate this time-to-productivity?

Firstly, by having an efficient hiring process that on-boards the right kind of people into the organization. Secondly, by giving the new hire all the support they need to become productive as quickly as possible. This support ranges from having all the information that the new rep needs to find their bearing quickly at their fingertips in a concize and easily accessible format. Importantly, this needs to include the corporate and what Chuck Carey, CEO of Compendian Inc calls 'tribal knowledge', i.e. the inherent know-how of how things work in an organization. Allow new reps to tap into these resources and they will ramp up faster and higher than ever before.

10. Symptom: Uncertainty surrounding how customers and prospects perceive the marketing effort

"More than half the information that Marketers have comes from their previous experience or their intuition," said The Harvard Business Review in 2013 in a paper called "Marketers Flunk The Big Data Test".

With an ever-increasing number of Marketing channels and platforms and a commensurate rise in the amount of content, it seems incredible that organizations are not exactly aware of what their target audience's response is to the content that they are spending so much time, money and effort on to create and disseminate.

Some businesses conduct focus groups or online surveys, but most of them do so only a few times a year and, due to the unreliability of survey response data, there is no guarantee that the results adequately reflect reality. After all, focus groups are known to change their minds, and surveys often only reflect the sentiments of a vocal minority of respondents, i.e. they may not paint a true-to-life picture.

Though some have touted it as the answer to all of Marketing's problems, marketing automation technology is not the savior some hoped it would be. It can only show which content is being viewed or downloaded from the website, not how it is perceived at the other end. It is little wonder that marketers are relying on their intuition and experience to fill the gaps in the knowns and the unknown unknowns (to paraphrase a line we are all familiar with).

Wouldn't it be great if Marketers had clarity around all their interactions with customers and prospects, their requirements, perceptions of marketing content and sales techniques? Armed with this knowledge, marketing teams would be much better equipped to support the sales teams fully and with confidence that their content and leads are hitting the mark instead of going to waste.

Chapter Takeaway

As we have seen, there are many symptoms of poor Sales+Marketing Collaboration. They can appear in isolation or in bunches, over time or overnight. No matter how far these symptoms have progressed, it is never too late to address these problems head on, and you hold all the tools you need to do so in your hand. As we will see in the next chapter, effective Sales+Marketing Collaboration is the key.

Peter Strohkorb

Chapter 8:
Sales+Marketing Collaboration
Makes All The Difference

My own research (available on www.peterstrohkorbconsulting.com) shows a vast gulf separating financially successful organizations from the less successful ones that correlates to the way they approach Sales+Marketing Collaboration. In other words, we were able to demonstrate *a direct correlation between Sales+Marketing Collaboration and financial business success.*

A staggering 81.5% of companies that reported a decrease in sales revenue in the previous year operate across separate sales and marketing silos.

Furthermore, growth organizations are, by and large, those that hold vastly more formal meetings between their sales and marketing teams than non-growth organizations, with an astounding average of 24% of the less successful ones admitting that they meet either "never" or only "annually" (presumably at the start-of-year sales kick-off). Perhaps unsurprisingly, more than 65% of large companies in which sales and marketing departments reportedly meet either "never" or "annually" reported decreasing revenue.

Organizations that said they had been unable to grow their revenue over the previous 12 months also seemed to have a sizeable gap between their sales and marketing teams in terms of what they thought was most important to growing sales results.

Marketing teams in less successful companies overwhelmingly reported that nurturing leads for Sales was their top priority. In more successful organizations, it was promotional activities and lead generation that marketing teams tended to select as their top priorities.

The story was similar when we turned our focus to sales teams in successful organizations: there tended to be more substantial overlap between Sales and Marketing. Far more frequently than they did so in less successful companies, the sales teams in the better performers in the study reported that the qualifying of sales leads was an important objective for the sales department.

This source of this perception gap is relatively obvious once you start to look at collaborative trends and how they relate to success. Less successful organizations are often those with separate performance metrics in each department. In other words, less successful organizations do not support objective alignment between the sales and marketing functions through joint metrics and KPIs. Since they are such an obvious place of overlap and often a source of friction between Sales and Marketing, sales leads are a great place to start the Sales/Marketing alignment process.

In 2014 <u>Accenture</u> found in a report, called "Top-Five Focus Areas for Improving Sales Effectiveness Initiatives" (<u>http://www.accenture.com/SiteCollectionDocuments/PDF/Accenture-Top-Five-Improvements-Sales-Effectiveness.pdf</u>) that more than 50% of the leads that Sales pursues are self-generated, with the remaining half split between customer referrals and leads that are generated by Marketing. Incidentally, this isn't due to a lack of marketing-originated leads being fed into the pipeline or the funnel – quite the contrary. The issue is not with quantity – it's with quality.

According to a joint study conducted by <u>Vorsight and the Bridge Group</u> (<u>http://blog.bridgegroupinc.com/blog/tabid/47760/bid/43186/Sales-Speaks-Perceptions-Ponderings-on-Marketing-Leads.aspx</u>), sales departments that were surveyed felt that almost 70% of the sales leads that Marketing fed into the sales pipeline were sub-par. 70% of their prospects were neither positioned, nor inclined to purchase at the time of contact. In other words, from a salesperson's perspective, more than two thirds of the leads that are being fed into the pipeline or funnel are practically useless. More than half of reps surveyed reported that less than 25% of marketing-generated leads were in their so-called "sweet spot".

One way to make broader consensus possible is to institute solid lead scoring practices. Only 40% of the companies that participated in the Vorsight/Bridge Group study were using lead scoring, so it is quite possible that the absence of practical tools that can help Marketing fully qualify leads in a way that Sales understands and appreciates may be at the root of the issues surrounding lead generation and acceptance.

In order to put a lead-scoring system in place, though, we need to bridge a sizeable definition gap first. The evidence that this gap exists (and is causing problems) is everywhere. I have seen marketing teams that consider someone's business card a lead (clearly setting the bar too low). On the other hand, I have heard salespeople say, "I only want sales leads when the customer is purchase-ready now!" (clearly, this is setting the bar too high).

In reality, of course, the bar needs to be set somewhere between these too extremes, neither too high, nor too low – in the sales lead 'Goldilocks Zone' if you will.

Technology vendors have been quick to don the cape and tights, claiming they have the solution to all of the issues surrounding definitions and lead scoring. They have created a defined series of process steps that are shared by Sales and Marketing which aim to eliminate the 'No-Man's Land' in the middle of the funnel, which is illustrated below.

According to this school of thought, Marketing first generates and then nurtures the sales leads up to a mutually agreed-upon point in the pipeline. Once that point has been reached, Marketing hands the lead over to Sales for follow up. This gives us two new sets of definitions: Marketing-Qualified Leads (MQLs) and Sales-Accepted Leads (SALs). While this approach is a good start, it is not the complete solution that some are claiming it to be. Sales and Marketing are retreating into their respective definitions and using them to deflect responsibility. What's worse, it seems that they're still not speaking the same language: MQLs seem to be largely focused on relationship quality and revenue potential, whereas SALs often focus purely on revenue conversion. Clearly, alignment along process lines does not automatically produce collaboration between Sales and Marketing.

Misaligned Sales Funnel

Something extremely important has been left out of the equation.

The latest data from CSO Insights suggests that, while there has been improvement in the last few years, more than 50% of organizations still lack a formal definition as to what constitutes a 'qualified lead' (http://www.csoinsights.com/ Publications/Shop/Sales-Performance-Optimization). As might be expected, having a formal and agree-upon definition in place strongly correlates to higher conversion rates. Those with a formal definition in place had conversion rates some 50% higher than those without any kind of concrete definition.

This is a solvable issue, yet we find that many organizations seem poorly equipped to address this misaligned sales funnel without outside help.

Here is a simplified illustration of the misalignment between Sales and Marketing teams as it pertains to the generation, nurturing, management and reporting of sales leads.

Before even attempting to bring Sales and Marketing together, many of the more successful organizations begin by adjusting their sales force KPIs so as to bring their sales departments into lockstep with their marketing teams. Aberdeen Group reports that 72% of best-in-class companies have a team-oriented approach toward sales performance management (http://www.aberdeen.com/Aberdeen-Library/8787/RA-sales-performance-management.aspx). This number drops to less than 50% among those at or below the average in terms of performance. Tying compensation to team performance assures that those who are finding success are making sure to share their strategies with their colleagues.

This does not, however, completely lift the crucial burden of personal sales quotas, which, as Jason Robinson of Digital Bridge recently pointed out, remain the primary concern for salespeople (not, as many marketers seem to think, conversion rates). Personal sales quotas remain a significant factor in Sales performance, so it would be unwise to make KPIs broadly collective (http://www.the-digital-bridge.com/2014-05-14/jrobinson/hey-b2b-marketers-sales-doesnt-care-conversion-rates/).

Again as per Aberdeen, the best-in-class performers are those that can strike the finest balance between team and individual performance through collective goal setting and constructive Sales Manager/sales rep relationships.

If collaboration is the eventual goal (and it should be), the lone-wolf attitude that is so typical of salespeople (as well as the collective 'go-it-on-our-own' attitude prevalent in sales departments) needs to make way in favor of a more cooperative mindset.

Chapter Takeaway

We inspected the cooperative mindset between Sales and Marketing and looked more closely at the areas of sales lead generation and management. Importantly, we discovered that alignment along process lines does not automatically result in collaboration. This discovery will play an important role throughout the implementation of the OneTEAM Method™.

Peter Strohkorb

Chapter 9:
Trends that are Reshaping the Sales World

By now, you should have a good idea whether or not collaborative issues may be impeding your organization's progress in today's highly competitive marketplace. Before we jump headfirst into how to implement the various collaborative strategies that make up the OneTEAM Method™, it is first necessary to understand the root causes of unsynchronized practices in today's organizations. These causes have much to do with how sales and marketing have evolved as disciplines over the last few decades.

Tracing this evolution will help us understand not only what twenty-first-century sales and marketing departments are facing but also why they find themselves unable or unwilling to address the issues that are keeping them from effective collaboration. Each side has issues to be addressed and redressed in order to move forward in an aligned and mutually beneficial way.

This chapter and the next one will deal, respectively, with the changing worlds of sales and marketing and the frictions that have sprung up thanks to the constantly shifting sands of early-twenty-first-century

business practices. Collaboration can resolve present frictions and help avoid future ones, but only when would-be collaborators know the obstacles that they are facing. Let's begin with Sales.

1. The New Sales Paradigm

First, it is important to understand that the world of sales is not what it once was. Digital disruption has pretty much forced both sales and marketing departments to adjust to the new world that both sellers and buyers now inhabit.

"The sales profession is in the midst of a radical change. Simple sales are inexorably moving to the Internet. The selling that remains is sophisticated and demanding. The salesperson of the future will become a business equal of the customer, a creative problem-solver and a value creator. These changes demand a high level of professionalism."

Professor Neil Rackham, one of the pioneers of modern research into sales performance and methodology.

This means that the tried and true sales methods of old are being overthrown in favor of softer, advisory approaches. At the same time, hitherto proven marketing techniques – especially those that relied on print media to communicate with customers – are adapting in ever-changing ways to massively popular digital platforms like Twitter, LinkedIn, Pinterest, Facebook, and others, some of which are still emerging.

This change to the way that marketing is conducted has profoundly influenced the way that sales are made as well. In particular, it has created a new class of customers that is more responsive to the techniques that used to be applied almost exclusively in the B2C (business-to-consumer or retail) world. These techniques are now becoming more prevalent in the B2B (business to-business or corporate) world. Combine this with the advent of data-driven marketing and big data analytics – both of which are also being felt in both sales and marketing departments – and you have a myriad of changes that are rippling through today's organizations.

Charting a course through these unclear waters has resulted in a wide range of experimentation into sometimes-unconventional practices – some of them successful and some of them not. Not the least among them is the practice of extending the paradigm of process-specific alignment to a more holistic paradigm of true collaboration between Sales and Marketing.

As Sales and Marketing adapt to new market realities and opportunities, they are often presented with a choice regarding their operational structure: either they continue to operate in discrete silos or they adapt to cooperate in ways that will not only make them more alert to their changing markets and customers, but will also allow them to become increasingly nimble in terms of adapting to the shifting market trends of the future. Organizations that use collaborative strategies to address the long-standing complaints of Sales about Marketing and vice versa will be powerfully equipped to compete in, and even dominate, their markets in the years and decades to come.

Those who doggedly refuse to release their grip on the sales methodology and terminology of yesteryear (which we'll turn to next) will be those that will be left in their more nimble competitors' dust.

2. The Gradual Obsolescence of the Old Sales Cycle

Previously, whether a customer would buy from an organization or its competitor depended almost entirely on the sales rep and his or her ability to build and maintain relationships with potential customers. The best salespeople were those who were able to constantly expand and persuade those within this sphere of influence. Salespeople thus propelled the selling process forward (or, in the case of poor salespeople, stalled the process or even sent it backwards).

We used diagrams such as the one here to describe the stages in this process that we called either the Sales Cycle or the Selling Cycle.

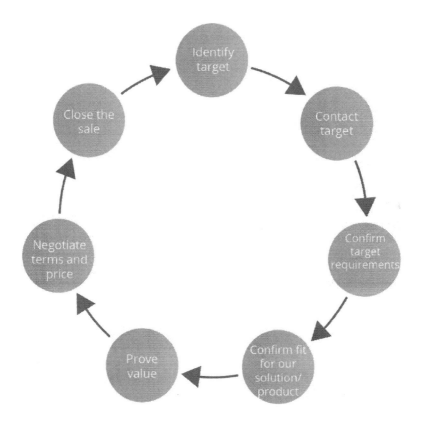

We liked to describe it as a *cycle* because we thought that as soon as we had finished making a sale, a new potential customer (a 'suspect') would be waiting at the top of the cycle and we would begin an identical customer-winning process with them, thus converting them into a new prospect. Also, when upselling was a possibility, the same customer could go through the sales cycle multiple times so that their potential as a customer could be maximized.

We also used these descriptors to measure sales progress and estimate the likely interval between stages in the cycle for reporting and forecasting purposes – otherwise known as the 'Contact to Cash' process. Potential customers are re-named at each stage: initially, they are targeted within their pre-defined market segment as 'suspects', approached by salespeople as 'prospects', and, once they have made their first purchase, they are, of course, customers'. You are probably familiar with the concept of the Sales Funnel or the Leaky Funnel: suspects are fed into the wide end of the funnel; some leak out, leaving the prospects behind. Some of these leak out again; finally, the remainder become buyers.

The Sales Cycle, with its organizationally inside-out perspective and language, was utterly vendor-centric. The power to move the sales process through its various stages was largely attributed to the sales rep, not to the prospect. Consequently, sales consultants and sales training vendors offered a myriad of sales techniques that could, they said, rapidly accelerate the sales cycle.

This was the halcyon era of "objection handling" and of "closing techniques," and of more comprehensive, market-research-based programs, such as Neil Rackham's "SPIN Selling" and Miller-Heiman's "Blue Sheet," "Gold Sheet," etc. plans. But informed buyers and their online research have disrupted the old Selling Cycle, creating a new purchasing paradigm, to which twenty-first-century sellers must adapt. Let's turn now to this new purchasing paradigm – the Buyer's Journey.

3. The Buyer's Journey (Buyer's Perspective)

As the illustration below makes clear, when it comes to the Buyer's Journey there is distinct criticality for the vendor around the timing of contact and the messaging to the suspect or prospect. In other words, it is now critical to be proactive, to send the right messages and information and, importantly, to do so at precisely the right time. Vendors now need to be seen by buyers as experts in their field and they need to stand out from the crowd in order to be noticed and accepted by the buyer on their journey.

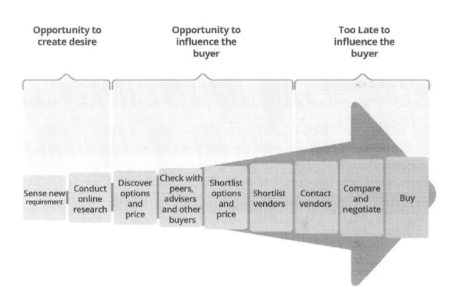

Early in the Buyer's Journey, vendors have a narrow window of opportunity to create a sense of desire/demand/need for their offering in a suspect's mind. This is the time where Marketing is most likely to play the biggest part in attracting new business as it can utilize its armory of channels and positioning messages to help suspects to discover our products and services over those of our competitors.

In the days of the Sales Cycle, a suspect contacted sales reps to obtain more information on a product or service. However, in the era of the Buyer's Journey, the buyer follows a very different trajectory. They are most likely to go online to conduct their own research, examining – often in meticulous detail – what the market is offering. Promotional materials (marketing collateral) play a part in this, but so do independent reviews and test reports.

Content marketing (which I'll discuss in much greater detail in the next chapter when we take a closer look at the Marketing landscape) is playing a large and still-expanding role in these early stages of the Buyer's Journey, and these effects are passing downstream to Sales. Sales reps who answer the phone are no longer expected to inform the client, at least not to the degree they once did. What the potential customer is seeking is not broad strokes but clarification. This means that sales reps are now expected to possess not only high-level selling skills but also a wide range of subject matter knowledge.

Any reluctance or inability on the part of the sales rep to provide the information that the buyer is after (i.e. instant value-add) will likely lead to the buyer continuing their journey with another organization.

The Buyer's Journey is, make no mistake, far less predictable and controllable than any of the purchasing paradigms that predate it. Just one disgruntled buyer is enough to spread the message far and wide and to poison the well. Bad reputations go viral in a heartbeat and the entire organization may have to expend untold energies on damage control.

Numerous studies have shown that by the time a buyer is ready to contact a vendor they have completed somewhere between 60% and 90% of their decision-making process. That means that by this time they have already whittled down their list of prospective vendors to a short-list. It is absolutely crucial that, at this time of the buyer transitioning from focusing on Marketing's messaging to sales rep contact, the handover is seamless and that both Sales and Marketing speak with one and the same voice. So much as a sniff of inconsistency and credibility can be damaged and the sale can be lost.

The global IT consulting firm <u>Accenture</u>'s market research (<u>http://www.accenture.com/SiteCollectionDocuments/PDF/Accenture-Top-Five-Improvements-Sales-Effectiveness.pdf</u>) has also shown that customer wants and needs are growing apace with their degree of connectivity. This is particularly true for tech-savvy buyers. At each and every touch point with the organization, customers expect added value and independent advice that is based on the vendor's thought leadership, and it must be consistent and transparent in every way.

Let me make this point in no uncertain terms:

Sales+Marketing Collaboration has become mission-critical. Allowing Sales and Marketing to speak different languages with buyers and the market at large can put the financial security of the entire organization at risk. Without collaboration, buyers lose respect for, and interest in, the vendor. When they walk, through the power of social media they can (and often will) motivate other to do the same. It's game over.

Now that we've looked at the Buyer's Journey from the buyer's perspective, let's turn to the same journey, but this time from the perspective of the vendor.

4. The Buyer's Journey (Vendors' Perspective)

The most obvious difference in the way that vendors are approaching today's buyers is *where* vendors are attempting to intercept buyers in the midst of their journey. Visibility is not as easy to find as it once was (when, for instance, print media could be relied upon to reach a wide swath of potential customers). Niche markets and segments are the new targets for visibility – particularly when these areas are rich in customers in the early stages of their journey. These are the buyers that today's vendors are focusing all of their efforts to intercept. Effective and on-point messaging all the way from the epiphany stage (i.e. their identification of a need or requirement) to the end of the consideration/research process is now seen as the best way to win (and keep) their attention.

In 2012, ITSMA reported that over 68% of B2B technology buyers identified this stage as the one in which they preferred to be contacted by sales reps (https://www.itsma.com/research/results-from-itsma-how-buyers-consume-information-survey-2012/). This is where salespeople can take on the crucial advisory role that sophisticated buyers are responding to, and are even actively seeking. While they were assembling research for their recent, cutting-edge sales manual, *The Collaborative Sale* Keith M. Eades and Timothy T. Sullivan found that vendors who engage with buyers at these early stages in their journey were five times more likely to win business than those who waited for buyers to initiate contact (http://www.amazon.com/The-Collaborative-Sale-Solution-Selling/dp/1118872428).

Simply put, informed customers are raising the bar that they then expect vendor company reps to clear for them. As shown in the illustration vendors need to become more proactive in charting the journey for the buyer to follow all the way to a successful sale, and beyond.

The Buyers' Journey from the Vendors' Perspective

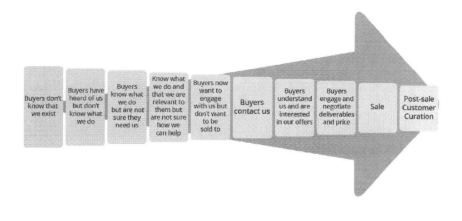

| Buyers don't know that we exist | Buyers have heard of us but don't know what we do | Buyers know what we do but are not sure they need us | Know what we do and that we are relevant to them but are not sure how we can help | Buyers now want to engage with us but don't want to be sold to | Buyers contact us | Buyers understand us and are interested in our offers | Buyers engage and negotiate deliverables and price | Sale | Post-sale Customer Curation |

Since salespeople used to be the ones who were most immediately engaging with their customers in the age of the Sales Cycle, they have now been the first to experience the challenges of this newly raised bar. The vendors who are having the most success are those who increase the run-up to this bar by shifting their focus to catching buyers' attention early in their journey. When it is a high-value product or a complex solution that is on the table, sales have never been easy to make, but increasingly informed buyers have compounded this difficulty for salespeople. One thing is sure: addressing savvy twenty-first-century customers requires sales techniques that are more sophisticated by far than those that were successful as little as a decade or two ago.

The relatively recent vocabulary shift to the Buyer's Journey underscores the need for a sales process that empathizes with the customer – seeing the sales process through their eyes – and fortifies the points at which the customer engages with sales reps or marketing-generated content. Digital Age buyers are armed with a different set of questions, some of which are catching unprepared organizations off guard:

- Do you know what my challenges are?

- What do you know about my competitors?

- What do you know about your competitors and my relationships with them?

- What ROI (Return on Investment) can I expect?

- What don't I know?

- Besides ROI, how are you adding value?

Each one of these questions represents an opportunity for sales reps to demonstrate the consultative and customer-centric approach that buyers are now looking for. However, while the Buyer's Journey offers opportunities, it also harbors its own set of challenges.

First of these is being able to gather, assess and act upon customer feedback. A 2014 research report by Aberdeen Group showed that best-in-class performers were those that consistently focused their resources in a customer-centric way, i.e. the ones that are opening feedback channels and who are meticulously managing the actionable data that lies therein (http://research.aberdeen.com/1/SR/April2014/0663-9000-RP-VoC-OM-AP-NSP-Final.pdf).

According to Accenture in a very interesting paper, called "Connecting The Dots On Sales Performance" (http://www.accenture.com/au-en/Pages/insight-connecting-dots-sales-performance.aspx), 67% of these best-in-class performers enabled and encouraged customer feedback at every touch point, whereas only 46% of leader-trailing organizations did the same. The importance of the new customer's voice cannot be overstated. More than anything, the new customer wants to feel that their feedback influences the way they are approached, addressed and acted upon by the seller.

According to Bob Apollo of Inflexion Point, today's time-poor buyers are beginning to feel that yesterday's sales model is a waste of their time (http://www.inflexion-point.com/Blog/bid/67962/B2B-Sales-and-Marketing-Is-Misalignment-Taking-10-Off-Your-Sales):

- 33% say they are regularly presented with too much information that is not useful to their search for a solution that suits their needs

- 29% complain about a lack of relevance to their specific situation

- 24% say that the information provided fails to address the needs of all the members of the buying team

- 23% feel that there simply isn't enough truly educational content

- 23% believe that the information provided isn't in a form they can share with others

According to Prelytix, prospects are engaging vendors only after having completed almost 60% of their decision-making process (http://www.prelytix.com/reality-b2b-sales-process-infographic/).

Others put this figure as high as 80%, meaning that by the time the buyer makes first contact with the vendor the customer has often already covered most of the ground that used to be the territory of salespeople. Buyers are initiating contact with sales reps merely to verify what they've learned through their own research. It's no surprise, therefore, that as much as 63% of sales are going to the first vendor with which customers are engaging.

Not only are vendors finding new customers an increasingly rare species in competitive markets, customer loyalty is harder than ever to obtain. The reasons for this change are, for the most part, reasonably predictable.

In a 2012 IDC survey more than half of the buyer's surveyed said they'd switch vendors due to a lack of follow up (http://www.idc.com/eagroup/download/accelerating-new-buyers-journey.pdf).

This means that there obviously needs to be a great deal of strategic alignment between what Sales and Marketing promise and what the organization delivers.

This consistency is expected in follow-up, but it is also demanded at every touch point in the pipeline. Organizations that can deliver a uniform experience from first touch point to last are those that are most likely to pull away from their competitors in leaps and bounds. Whether it is the sales experience, the marketing presence, or their after-sale service, new customers are highly attuned to corporate culture, and they want to feel that, from the top down, every facet of the organization is aligned, and aligned to their needs at that. Even a slight deviation is often enough to make prospects and customers start exploring other options. Ubiquitous vendors and abundant choice brought on by the Internet means that just one bad customer experience at any of the touch points – or even the perception of a bad experience – has viral potential.

We now understand that a single mismanaged touch point, one poorly aligned Marketing to Sales hand-off, even an off-message rep can poison the well in an instant. Effective inter-departmental alignment can dramatically reduce or even eliminate such inconsistent customer experiences and thus avoid disaster.

Finally, the new breed of tech-savvy customers demand a technologically sophisticated, convenient and information-rich interface from the organizations they are considering doing business with. This is putting substantial pressure on vendors to respond to these expectations with an expanded social media presence, mobility options, data analytics, and cloud capability (SMAC), but also on the new breed of sales rep, who are as much subject matter experts as they are company representatives and solution-oriented salespeople.

As we will see later on, technology is not in itself the answer, but it is definitely one of the doors through which customers might beat a hasty retreat if vendors should fail to meet their expectations.

Digital-age customers undoubtedly expect sophistication, but the higher the purchase price, the more they expect that sophistication to manifest itself in organizational service, not just in technology per se. The longer the likely tenure of the post-sale relationship (e.g. when buying a new IT backend system or outsourcing service), the more scrutiny the vendor will come under and the more they will need to respond with timely and relevant information and personalized service. It is easy to see how there is a fine balance to be struck here and that every organization may strike it differently.

The most successful organizations that I have encountered are invariably those that have adapted their people, practices and technologies so that they can look authoritative at every stage of the Buyer's Journey and with a high degree of uniformity. In large organizations, it is not unusual for management to devote entire teams to 'CX' or Customer Experience. These organizations can boast people and technologies that are nimble and adaptable; they are able to deliver a consistently high-quality customer experience, and their customers are rewarding their efforts.

5. The New Salesperson

Today's information-rich buyers are increasingly unresponsive to yesterday's sales techniques. This is making it more difficult than ever for salespeople to get through to prospects and decision makers on the phone, let alone to get them to attend physical business events or trade shows. Yet, without that person-to-person contact, they are unable to gauge prospects' level of interest through traditional means such as body language and other non-verbal cues.

As so many salespeople watch their performance numbers ebb, they face a dilemma: either they adjust to the market by learning an entirely new set of skills (including how to work in concert with Marketing), or they continue to rely on those customers (an endangered species) who still seek out pre-millennial, old-fashioned pitchmen. Naturally, the wise money is on the former.

To put it mildly, the information-saturated, point-and-click world that is the Internet has forever changed customers and their buying behaviors. The buyer has taken control of the buying process away from the traditional sales rep. In the days of the Sales Cycle, it was the sales rep who was in a hurry to close the sale and move on. These days the buyer and the sales rep have swapped places. Today's buyer is the one who is in a hurry to get to the satisfaction point of a purchase – once, that is, they have identified a need and researched their vendor options.

Sales training vendors have reacted to the new paradigm with a myriad of supposedly new training programs. To be fair, twentieth- and early-twenty-first-century sales training programs – thorough products of their time – worked well in the days of the Sales Cycle (provided they were implemented and managed appropriately). Now that the paradigm has shifted, there has been no small amount of scrambling on the part of sales trainers, who are doing their level best to hammer some old square pegs into some very new round holes. Yesterday's techniques are being rebranded or adapted to supposedly suit the market's new realities, but the changes seem mostly at the level of language.

In their essence, sales strategies (some of them now decades old) have remained unchanged. At the risk of potentially doing my sales training peers a disservice, it is my perception that the supposedly new and disruptive sales techniques are really little more than reinvented variants of yesteryears' methods. A little more modishly dressed up, presented and packaged, but essentially the same. To me they look suspiciously like they are still channeling the basic elements of Neil Rackham's SPIN method from 30 years ago. The difference being that we no longer expect our prospects to answer a multitude of situation-exploring questions before we attempt to sell them something. Prospects these days are far less patient and they expect modern reps who have done their homework.

The days of the charismatic but tactical salesperson are getting behind us, particularly in B2B sales. A winning personality still goes a long way, but today's buyers aren't looking for slick pitchmen. What they are looking for is a subject matter expert, somebody who knows exactly why buyers are solution-hunting in the first place, someone who has insight into their situation and solutions that are tailored to their most pressing issues. They don't want to hear, "I'll get back to you on that." They want answers, and they want them now. Buyers are no longer looking for a sales rep; they are looking for an advisor. After they have conducted all their own research, they want to deal with someone who knows even more than they do about the problem they are trying to solve and the offering that they are most interested in. A poorly prepared or under-informed sales rep is likely to get very short shrift indeed. Don't get me wrong, there are still buyers out there – particularly B2C buyers - who prefer to walk into a shop and buy from a sales rep on the shop floor. However, the trend is moving away from this long-familiar scenario.

During a guest lecture to the Executive MBA class of the Sydney Business School, I posed the following question to the attendees: How did you conduct your last major purchase? One of them described how he bought a big screen TV simply by walking into a popular retail store and asking the first rep sell them one. A small handful of other respondents cited similar or identical buying behaviors, all of them in a B2C context.

The vast majority of attendees, however, followed a very different path. To cite a single example, one lady in the front of the room said she had recently purchased a new family car. She described how she first went online to explore which cars were available that covered her needs within her price range. Then she went on to look at online vehicle test report sites and checked her impressions against the opinions of her friends, acquaintances and peers. Finally, she looked online at the personal perceptions and experiences of people who had previously purchased the same model that she was now considering.

By the time she was ready to speak to a sales rep she had already decided, not only what brand and model she wanted, but also what color it was to be, what options she required and what price she was prepared to pay. She told the class that she would have been quite prepared to even order the car online if that option had been available to her and that pretty much the only reason she and her husband visited a dealership was to take a test-drive in the car that they had decided to buy.

In summary, she had completed far more than 80% of her decision-making process before she contacted the car dealership. All that the salesperson could do was to take her order and to deliver the car. Can you see how the poor rep in the showroom had next to no control over the sale? All the power remained in the hands of the buyer. That is the power of the Buyer's Journey.

We are now seeing signs that the above B2C mindset is starting to infiltrate the B2B sales world. Storytelling and sales presentations remain important pillars of the selling game, but they are increasingly trumped by situationally adept consultational skills that are complemented by extensive market insight and specialist solution expertise.

In the aforementioned IDC survey buyers' preference for this kind of intimate understanding of customer wants/needs and solution-oriented problem-solving skills outstripped old-fashioned knowledge of product features and accumulated sales experience.

Modern information-rich pre-sales consultants are driving future sales. Even call centers are adjusting the way that their telemarketers or tele-prospectors work. Having traditionally been the light infantry of sales teams, they are changing their tactics, honing in on breaks in the line opened up, not so much by cold calling, but by highly targeted marketing campaigns. There is focus like never before on working the trigger points, i.e. those points at which the prospects' buying journey and the vendors' sales content or expert staff intersect.

At these intersections, the savviest of today's vendors are erecting what I call 'beacons of expertise', which vendors are using to attract buyers during the online research phase of their journey. These take a variety of shapes: webinars, white papers, interviews, and sophisticated multi-channel social media engagements. While in the past these have largely been the exclusive domains of marketers, more and more salespeople are beginning to cross into these unfamiliar but bountiful waters. At the very least, salespeople are learning to turn their own familiarity with the same materials that their customers are encountering online to their advantage, especially when the prospect reaches out and initiates contact, perhaps with questions that relate to this content. If the salesperson is able to display much more than just a passing familiarity with the subject matter, they can start to assist the prospect through the final stages of the Buyer's Journey and direct them away from competitor offerings towards their own.

However, not all salespeople are ready to adjust to the new world order. As sales managers who have been around since the days of Palo Alto Laboratories and the innovations that arrived in the 1970s can tell you, the reality is that many senior salespeople are little inclined to adjust their methods or mindset to fit new paradigms. This reluctance to metamorphose into the new sales environment is a substantial factor in the diminishing bottom line for many sales-based organizations.

Many of my executive clients tell me that they need to evolve from a product-centric organization to a customer-centric, solutions-oriented one, but that their own reps are unable or unwilling to make that transition.

The Challenges facing Sales Reps

"67% of sales professionals do not achieve their personal sales quota."
The TAS Group

TOO MANY DISTRACTIONS ?

"Less than 35% of a sales rep's time is spent selling."
CSO Insights

"CRM tool adoption rate is less than 50 percent."
CSO Insights

"~60% of sales pipeline is stuck with no decision pending."
Qvidian

"The average sales person spends ~7 hours per week looking for relevant information to prepare for sales calls."
Forrester Research

NOT ENOUGH SUPPORT ?

"Only 25% of sales leads and collateral that Marketing creates is ever used by Sales teams."
IDC

"Fewer than 15 percent of organizations achieved improved win rates from implementing sales tools."
Accenture

"Almost 78% of newly hired sales reps take 6 months or longer to become fully proficient at selling."
Accenture

In one of the largest technology vendor organizations that I have worked with, management had come to realize that future sales margins were going to come from selling solutions, not hardware. They tried, as gently as possible, to move their sales reps into pushing software to go with the hardware as a kind of 'thin end of the wedge', something that could slowly but surely transition their selling practices more towards solution-selling. The prevailing attitude of the died-in-the-wool hardware sales reps, though, was that, "Software is only 10% of the revenue, but it is 90% of the trouble. I'd rather sell another piece of hardware (colloquially referred to as a 'box') than any software." The sad reality for this organization was that fewer than 20% of their reps were realistically capable of adapting to the new solution-selling paradigm. In no time at all, they were left without options. They were forced to transition out about 80% of their reps and sales managers and replace them with new blood. There's no way to sugarcoat this: the financial and emotional costs were immense.

Drastic as the move may have seemed to the terminated staff or to uninformed outsiders, it was absolutely necessary for the future prosperity of the organization. For the organization in question, adapting to the new paradigm meant an almost complete overhaul of their sales department.

The alternative is worse. Old-school sales techniques being applied to new-school customers manifests itself in closure rates plummeting, too many sales leads remaining unattended, and too may 'stuck deals' in the sales pipeline that are not moving forward.

Here are three things the most successful of the new-school salespeople are doing consistently and are doing well:

1) They are using social listening and in-depth research to catch buyers during their discovery and consideration phases
2) They are surprising and delighting potential buyers with data or insights that interrupt or divert their journey away from competitors
3) They are positioning themselves as subject matter experts and trusted advisors, rather than as sales reps

The first of these requires world-class communication between sales and marketing teams; the second demands significant dedication and flexibility on the part of salespeople, who need to broaden and deepen their scope if they are to adapt to today's customers and their needs; the third requires the ongoing development of new skills and aptitudes. The demand for sales consultants who fit this mold is far outstripping supply, making it more difficult than ever for organizations to get out ahead of the rapidly swinging pendulum, which is swinging towards a vital new breed of sales reps who are as much subject matter experts and consultative solution salesperson as they are company representatives. These twenty-first-century salespeople are the *avant garde* in the ongoing revolution of sales practices.

Chapter Takeaway

The world of sales has changed significantly over the last few years, and some of the boundaries are beginning to blur – not least of all, the boundary between Sales and Marketing. Clearly, significant challenges abound and only a collaborative mindset is the way of the future.

Chapter 10:
Trends that are Reshaping the World of Marketing

Just as we are seeing digital disruption in sales departments worldwide, the new breed of customers has forced marketing departments to follow the customers online. Increasingly, this means using a wide range of digital platforms (including social media) to reach their audience. In the last chapter, we briefly covered some of the ways that Marketing is taking the lead in the generation of new kinds of content (much of it online) that is being used to influence buyer's during the early stages of their journey. In this chapter we'll be looking at the changing world of marketing in much more detail, starting with changing budgets and what they tell us about the seismic shift in the way organizations are targeting today's highly informed and digitally savvy customers.

1. Changing Budgets

Some, including Katy Keim, CMO of Lithium Technologies, suggest that organizations should overhaul their sales and marketing budgets to reflect the new reality of market-savvy customers (http://www.lattice-engines.com/resources/ebooks/sales-marketing-alignment-guide). "[A] cold call," Keim says, "doesn't work anymore". Since these customers are walking themselves through so much of the buying process before they are initiating contact, "smart companies," she says, "[are] moving money from the Sales portfolio directly into the Marketing portfolio."

John Jantsch, in a 2014 interview with Dan Schawbel says much the same thing: "Salespeople are currently over-valued and over-compensated and marketing people are under-valued." (http://www.forbes.com/sites/danschawbel/2014/03/15/john-jantsch-why-sales-teams-must-have-a-marketing-mindset/).

While I wouldn't say that I agree entirely with either of these statements, it is fair to say that, even in B2B situations, Marketing is playing an increasing role thanks to the still-evolving Buyer's Journey.

Google Search Analytics bear this point out. Below are two graphs that illustrate the Google search trends for certain keywords over time, i.e. how often these keywords were searched for online over the last few years.

The first diagram shows the search trends for the keywords 'Advertising' and 'Marketing'. As you can see, these traditional marketing terms are trending downwards in terms of search frequency.

Now, let us look at what happens when we preface the keywords above with the prefix 'Digital':

As the trend lines in the two graphs above reflect, traditional marketing methods and digital marketing (represented by the keywords 'Digital Marketing' and 'Content Marketing') are moving into opposite directions. Marketing budgets are beginning to reflect this reality as well.

Back in 2012 Lisa Arthur predicted in a Forbes article that *"Five Years From Now, CMOs Will Spend More on IT Than CIOs Do."* Software-as-a-Service (SaaS) offerings and Big Data Analytics will only accelerate this trend (http://www.forbes.com/sites/lisaarthur/2012/02/08/five-years-from-now-cmos-will-spend-more-on-it-than-cios-do/).

IDC's Rich Vancil talks about the changing budgets in terms of MBR (Marketing Budget Ratio) and SBR (Sales Budget Ratio) (http://adage.com/article/btob/sharpen-pencils-8211-marketing-budget-season/284103/?btob=1).

He says, *"In a nutshell, you want to try to keep your MBR fairly constant. Ramp it up with revenue increase and walk it down with revenue decreases, but try to avoid dramatic swings in either direction."*

Trying to get to your final destination in one giant leap is rarely advisable. Keep everybody on board by giving them time to adjust to shifting budgets before making further changes.

Vancil continues: *"Think about the totality of Marketing plus sales costs. For a large tech vendor, we calculate an average MBR of 2.1 %, and a SBR of 8.5%, for a total of 10.6%. The best opportunity for Marketing and Sales productivity improvement continues to be at the intersection of these two functions."*

Unlike Vancil, I believe that Sales+Marketing Collaboration should not be applied only to a narrow set of pre-defined processes, but that it should become a pervasive modus operandi that encompasses all the touch points and overlaps between Sales and Marketing.

Back in 2011, Vancil also noted that, since 2009, those in control of marketing budgets have advocated an increasingly larger slice of the pie to digital marketing. In 2009, it was 12.6%, in 2010, 19.3%, and he projected those numbers to continue to rise to 26.4% by the end of 2011. The latest (2014) numbers from Econsultancy show that the trend, as predicted, continued unabated, with companies spending, on average, 38% of their marketing budgets on digital in 2014 (https://econsultancy.com/reports/marketing-budgets).

The ripple effect of this seismic budgetary shift is being felt in both sales and marketing departments. It is changing not only the way that brands are being managed, but also the way that sales and marketing organizational structures are reacting to this trend.

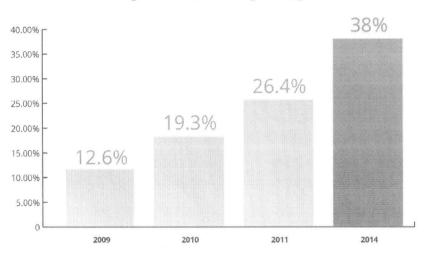

2. The Decentralization of Marketing

This old silo structure (a central marketing department and a geographically decentralized sales force) is giving way to a new structure, one that seeks to integrate sales and marketing functions along channel or competency lines.

Depending on the organization, this decentralization of the marketing function is taking effect in one of two significant ways: either in a vertical market sector or in a geographically delineated fashion. Once again, Marketing and Sales are being asked to give up their 'us vs. them' attitudes and to harmonize with each other along channel or competency lines. As we saw earlier, this is a response to emerging trends that are reshaping the way that salespeople are approaching, and are being approached, by customers.

Just as salespeople are facing new challenges (we discussed this at length in the last chapter) the same applies to marketers. The reality is that they are also coming under increasing pressure to perform, and to do so in tangible and measurable ways.

The following infographic illustrates these raised expectations:

The Challenges facing Marketers

"Up to 70% of Marketers in 2013 were not living up to the expectations of their CEOs"
The Fournaise Marketing Group

These expectations were:
• More sales-ready leads
• More market share
• More revenue

In light of these heightened expectations are marketing teams equipped to adequately support their sales counterparts? Do they have the necessary subject matter insight to provide the kind of content Sales needs to speak effectively with today's customers? With so much of the Buyer's Journey taking place online, is Marketing equipped with the kind of budgets and technologies it needs to best represent the organization? Is the organizational structure conducive to collaborative success?

It seems that, just like Sales, Marketing may also be struggling to adapt to the new trends. Some marketers are reporting that the market is evolving faster than their adaptive practices can run, leaving them with something of an innovation deficit.

I aim to address these questions below.

3.   The Tug-of-War Between Macro- and Micro-Marketing

Sales organizations with multinational or even global reach are re-orienting their sales efforts to better service their largest customers. Unprecedented global competition is pulling these large organizations in multiple directions: globally consistent service and branding are magnetic and marketable, but this can fall short of addressing the kind of market- and region-specific needs of customers. The most desirable clients, considering their plethora of options, are increasingly expecting or even demanding this kind of micro-focus through all of their touch points with the organization regardless of geography.

In the past, the drive for consistency tended to lead to centralized marketing departments (usually located at the corporate head office), which created and distributed material broadly to decentralized sales teams. Often, when the sales force is spread around the world, Marketing would be tempted simply to re-use the same content, merely translating it into the local language with little consideration paid to local culture, customs, beliefs and attitudes.

The pressures that twenty-first-century customers are exerting on salespeople are now being passed up the line to Marketing. Often to the surprise of the marketing team, local sales forces are resisting macro-marketing strategies. Regional- and customer-specific needs – so the argument goes – are being sacrificed on the altar of global brand consistency. The net effect of this drive for consistency is that salespeople often feel let down by Marketing and they feel the need to produce their own collateral that more adequately reflects the specific conditions in the market in which it will be used.

The lack of content control that this represents can have unexpected consequences. For instance, in an Australian subsidiary of a global, Japanese-headquartered technology firm, a sales rep stepped out of bounds, creating and presenting a brochure for a product that he thought the customer wanted and that he thought did exist. When it was discovered that the promised product did not in fact exist, there was a lot of back-pedaling and red faces all around.

This kind of disconnect between Sales and Marketing can also manifest itself in the opposite direction. In the Australian branch of a global, US-headquartered IT firm, a prospective customer asked a sales rep to visit them to discuss a new service offered by the organization. When the rep asked which particular service was of interest to the prospect, the answer came as something of a shock. The prospect showed him a nice glossy brochure (which the rep had never seen) of a service (which the rep had never heard of). After some embarrassing exchanges between the rep and the prospect, the rep made enquiries further afield. It turned out that the marketing department at the US head office had authorized the launch of an entirely new service in the rep's region, but somehow, head office had neglected to inform the Australian region's sales department.

This is just one example among many. The larger the organization, the more likely they have suffered from embarrassing and potentially relationship-killing interactions like this one.

During my time working at several regional offices of multinational organizations with headquarters based in the USA, we called this phenomenon "The world from coast to coast," referring to the often domestically focused outlook of many American organizations.

US-based marketers appear to be mostly unaware of how different people really are outside of the US – this is true even in countries that share English as a mother tongue. A great deal of my work in the US involved educating American marketers about the difference between consistency and sameness.

Consistency, to my way of thinking, means that the message is understood in the same way, independently of regional differences, whereas sameness as a marketing strategy is predicated on the mistaken belief that all cultures perceive meaning and formulate value identically.

At long last, this message seems to be sinking in. Forward-thinking organizations are striving to balance macro- and micro-marketing by decentralizing the marketing effort while retaining a centralized, brand-sensitive strategy that informs regional satellite offices without dictating to them.

Being sensitive to cultural differences is much easier when Sales and Marketing are collaboratively engaged, particularly across geographical regions. Salespeople on the front lines of foreign markets have a wealth of information to share and have already done some of the important groundwork in terms of dovetailing the micro-marketing needs and the macro-marketing vision of the organization. Also, head offices should never think of themselves as holding a monopoly on innovation. Some of the best ideas I have encountered and traced back to their source were originally conceived in regional sales offices and were then passed back up the stream to the global head office.

Like almost every aspect of twenty-first century business practices, there are software vendors offering supposed shortcuts. After a proliferation of CRM systems, a lot of organizations are now adding automation technology and, in particular, marketing automation, to their technology armory, but this is not something that should replace human insight into regional markets. As Sales and Marketing come into alignment, they can share market insight and real-world experience to create a much more vivid picture of the regional market than a silo approach could ever possibly hope to capture.

Also, marketing automation should never become a set-and-forget affair. I spoke to the Head of Marketing at a large financial services organization recently and he explained to me that, sometimes, geographically specific external factors, such as a fall in the currency exchange rate, or a bull run on that country's stock market, may necessitate a change in Marketing's focus and in the content that they promote. Technology needs to support this rapid adaptability, not stifle it.

4. Content Marketing and Inbound Marketing

Perhaps somewhat frivolously, I am using content marketing and inbound marketing as synonymous terms here. Some people prefer to call inbound marketing a subset of content marketing but, in the end, the idea is to attract the market's attention by publishing captivating content.

Due to the Buyer's Journey, consumers are going online to inform themselves of their options. By and large, today's buyers contact a vendor when they have reached or are very close to reaching a purchasing decision. Depending on whose research you subscribe to, it is said that between 50 and 80+ percent of buying decisions are already made by the time a consumer contacts a vendor, so it's no wonder that marketers are responding with techniques that are designed to attract the attention of the buyer *before* they have made this decision. Content marketing and inbound marketing have sprung up and flourished for precisely this reason.

It might be fair to ask what precisely I mean by 'content'? I define the term rather broadly so that it includes a heterogeneous mixture of both different kinds of materials and media types. Here's a selection of some of the terms that I would list under my definition of 'content':

News articles, success stories, testimonials, videos, newsletters, infographics, apps, websites, animations, blogs, e-books, podcasts, social media discussion forums, content sharing services, presentations, webinars, white papers, research reports, online publications, magalogues, etc.

Basically, any customer-facing information is, in my books, content.

What makes content and inbound marketing so revolutionary is that it turns on its head the relationship between Sales and the customer. Rather than targeting and pursuing customers using the customary channels, content/inbound marketing aims to establish an organization and its members as valuable resources, not of products or services, but of thought leadership. It aims to build relationships of trust and respect that can (and very often does) lead to productive business relationships.

This is a development that has come hand in hand with the advisor role that salespeople are playing. When Marketing-generated content demonstrates thought leadership, salespeople are, at times, able to take a more passive role than they once did. It may well be true that customers are coming to them in increasing numbers already convinced that the organization is the kind of partner that they are looking for. On the other hand, though, the traditional sales rep is increasingly becoming at least somewhat of a subject matter expert. Why is that? Because the buyer will have decided to contact the vendor that seems best to understand his or her problem and to offer the precise solution he or she is seeking. This, of course, places considerable pressure on the sales rep to be a subject matter expert, but the exceptional reps are beginning to clear this bar.

In a recent Sales+Marketing alignment seminar, John Jantsch, author of Duct Tape Marketing and Duct Tape Selling (http://www.ducttapemarketing.com/), highlighted the need for twenty-first-century marketers to use strategic networking and partnerships to position themselves and their organizations as thought leaders. Prudent marketers, Jantsch says, are aligning with non-competitive organizations, sponsoring events or contributing to industry research. The savviest of these marketers are aware of the major and minor industry journalists and trendsetters. Well-timed or targeted coverage that comes from non-competing parties like these can be invaluable to a brand.

I like this quote by Doug Kessler, Creative Director at Velocity Partners (http://uk.linkedin.com/in/dougkessler/en) , a UK-based content marketing agency: "*Traditional marketing talks at people. Content marketing talks to, and with, them.*"

That sums it up quite nicely for me.

The surging popularity of content marketing is leading to a re-evaluation on the part of marketing departments in terms of which strategy to adopt. Whilst some analysts, like those at the <u>Content Marketing Institute</u> claim that traditional marketing methods of all stripes are no longer effective, my own research and experience has made me reluctant to throw the baby out with the bathwater. All too often, people seem to be drawn in by the newest and shiniest thing. In my mind, content marketing should complement an existing marketing strategy, not replace it entirely (<u>http://contentmarketinginstitute.com/what-is-content-marketing/</u>).

Those of us old enough to remember have seen marketing trends come in with a bang and go out with a whimper – only to come back again dressed up in new clothes in another season. Just look at yo-yo business themes like insourcing vs. outsourcing or centralization vs. decentralization. It's no wonder I am cautious about declaring traditional methods dead before their time. For all the enthusiasm with which marketers seem to have embraced content marketing, I urge a degree of caution. Traditional marketing methods have breath in them yet. As it so often does, the pendulum may swing back, though when it does it is most likely we will end up, not with one or the other, but with a bouquet of content and media, old and new side by side.

Be that as it may, however, shying away from content or inbound marketing altogether will quickly leave you inhaling your competitors' exhaust fumes. There is strong evidence to show that content marketing, of all the recent marketing innovations, has the strongest legs. As of late 2014, 91% of B2B businesses that responded to the Content Marketing Institute's queries were using content marketing over a wide range of platforms to address their customers. More than half of those surveyed planned to devote more resources to content marketing in the coming year (http://contentmarketinginstitute.com/wp-content/uploads/2012/11/b2bresearch2013cmi-121023151728-phpapp01-1.pdf).

Again, as per the same Content Marketing Institute survey, best-in-class performers lead the way in terms of content marketing resource allocation: best-in-class organizations devote, on average, 46% of their marketing budget to content marketing; average performers 33%; least effective organizations 16%. As previously mentioned, there are predictions that say that by 2015 the IT budget of the CMO will exceed that of the CIO. For those who see their budgets grow in this way, much of the new funds will be spent producing and disseminating quality digital content.

Before leaping headfirst, though, there is something else to consider – something that is often referred to as 'the dark side of content marketing'. That something is content quality.

It seems that some content marketers operate according to the motto "quantity over quality". The enemy of content marketing is the content itself. For content marketing to be effective, it is vital that the content resonates powerfully with the target audience. Spamming whole market segments with trivial information and regurgitated platitudes is not what content marketing is meant to be.

Just put yourself into the shoes of a buyer who is looking for information on a particular product or service. If your prospects are looking for valuable information to help them make the right decision, how likely are they to be attracted to your organization if all you send them is shallow trivia? No matter how many times it may be repeated, content is not king. Only quality content can lay claim to that title.

Of course, not every organization has the kind of talented copywriters needed to create engaging and thought-provoking material. That is why there are all sorts of service providers and freelancers popping up to create and support content marketing strategies. Remember, the market is no fool. Always assume that your prospects are intelligent enough to know when they are being informed vs. when they are being pitched at. A single ham-fisted piece of ill-conceived content can kill a fledgling relationship in the short time it takes to read a few sentences or even just a subject line.

The key is to present the right content to the right audience at the right time. Successful content marketers understand that buyers have different needs at different stages in their journey. Content marketers create matrices of so-called 'buying personas' that are laid over the different stages in their Buyer's journey so that they can map what content should be presented to whom and, just as importantly, when. This relies in no small measure upon quality data and the sophisticated understanding of customer needs that emerges when this data is carefully scrutinized. Quality content in the wrong hands is as ineffective as inferior content is counter-productive in the right ones.

If that sounds like a lot of detailed work, that's because it is. It should come as no surprise that technology vendors have been quick to appear on the scene, offering their panacean solutions, most of which attempt to automate marketing. Placed in the right hands, marketing automation can indeed produce astounding results, but in the wrong ones it can fray prospects' nerves, or worse, destroy value.

Lazy content marketing looks a lot like spam on steroids, whereas clever content marketing can be a delicate balancing act along a four-dimensional tightrope, namely the Buyer's journey stage, the various personae, the (quality) content itself, and automation technology.

Finally, it's crucial that we don't forget that today's buyers are attracted to consistency and repulsed by its opposite. Content marketing that adopts a language or tone that poorly reflects the cultivated values throughout the organization will land like a lead balloon. Make sure that Marketing doesn't make promises with its content that Sales can't keep. Alignment at every level will substantially reduce the risks that this will occur.

5. New Platforms / Social Media Marketing

It has become commonplace for twenty-first-century organizations to maintain a social media presence, often on a wide range of platforms. YouTube, LinkedIn, Facebook, Instagram and Twitter are the more common ones, but there are dozens of other sites that marketing professionals are adding to their exposure arsenal. The so-called digital natives (i.e. millennials who grew up surrounded by mobile devices and other online technologies) expect businesses to offer and maintain a strong, multi-platform online presence.

B2B marketers are using social media to share their blog posts, product images, infographics, case studies, and white papers, and they are building brand awareness, increasing website traffic, and generating leads at a terrific rate when they can demonstrate sufficiently strong brand or thought leadership to interrupt the Buyer's Journey.

The savviest marketers are dispersing carefully curated content across multiple platforms. This is particularly important when targeting digital natives. In 2012, a Time Inc. study found that these young consumers switch media venues about 27 times per non-working hour (http://www.reuters.com/article/2012/04/09/idUS106537+09-Apr-2012+BW20120409).

Betsy Frank, Chief Research and Insights Officer for Time Inc., commented on these findings: "In order to keep Digital Natives engaged, content creators and marketers will need to think differently. Grabbing them from the beginning is essential, as is content they can snack on, and offering multiple access points to every story." Content must be at once provocative and widely dispersed through the major platforms (Facebook, Twitter, LinkedIn, and YouTube). Smaller (but growing) platforms like Foursquare, Tumblr, Pinterest and Instagram can be surprisingly productive as well. Though the consumer pools to be found there are shallower, users who frequent these sites are often active on dozens of platforms, and, no matter what the product, service, or market, twenty-first century customers are looking for brand consistency. By being everywhere, and everywhere consistently, marketers can build a powerfully magnetic online presence.

The graphic here is courtesy of CMI/Marketing Profs. While the data is a few years old, it illustrates quite nicely how content marketers are using multiple social media sites to broadcast their content (http://www.marketing.org/files/public/2015_B2B_Research_Final.pdf).

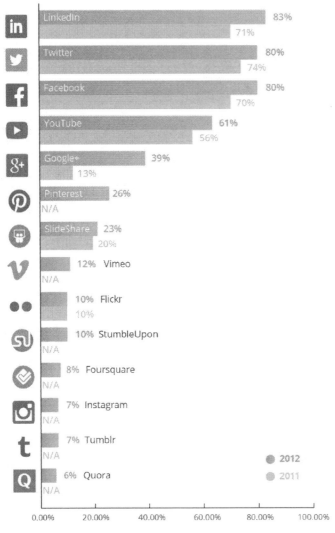

Percentage of B2B Marketers
Who Use Various Social Media Sites
to Distribute Content

	2012	2011
LinkedIn	83%	71%
Twitter	80%	74%
Facebook	80%	70%
YouTube	61%	56%
Google+	39%	13%
Pinterest	26%	N/A
SlideShare	23%	20%
Vimeo	12%	N/A
Flickr	10%	10%
StumbleUpon	10%	N/A
Foursquare	8%	N/A
Instagram	7%	N/A
Tumblr	7%	N/A
Quora	6%	N/A

2013 B2B Content Marketing Benchmarks-North America: CMI/MarketingProfs

It can be very tempting for marketers to pivot their attention entirely towards the new shiny thing that is online platforms. There is, however, anecdotal evidence to suggest that a degree of caution is warranted here.

After a massively successful, multi-platform and multi-media campaign, Bernadine Buys of Clear Creek Communications was surprised to learn that the majority of the customers surveyed were drawn to the offer through print media (https://www.ntca.org/online-exclusives/print-marketing-still-an-effective-tool.html) Print media is, of course, the most traditional and also the most expensive option, but that doesn't mean that it should be ignored in favor of the new marketing platforms. The ROI on an engaging print media campaign might be higher than you think. With all the frenzy surrounding content marketing and social media marketing, it is hardly surprising that a number of today's marketing professionals – especially those who are digital natives themselves – regard traditional marketing as yesterday's news. Don't pay too much attention to what the kids are saying, though. The savviest marketers are those who are recognizing that a mix of old and new is the best way to meet buyers wherever they are and through whatever media they would like to be approached.

6. New Tools and Data

So much of the contact between customers and organizations is digital in nature that marketing and sales tactics alike are moving into multiple digital channels.

The twenty-first-century marketer or salesperson worth his or her salt is learning to understand what Steven Woods calls "digital body language" (http://digitalbodylanguage.blogspot.com/2009/01/book-digital-body-language.html). Assisted by cloud-based and millennial-minded data mining and analysis technology, marketers are beginning to lift and learn from the digital fingerprints that are left behind whenever a prospect consumes, shares, comments on, or otherwise engages with digital content.

"For the first time," says Woods, "Marketing [is] able to glean and provide detailed, metric-backed insights into buyers and their goals." This kind of customer insight is driving some of the strongest B2B performers as specific insights of this kind allow marketing and sales teams to intercept the buyer's journey more effectively. Even when armed with knowledge and content tailor-made to the customer's needs, it is nonetheless difficult to predict the behaviors of today's customers accurately, particularly when they are moving relatively anonymously through digital channels. Technology is trying to come to the rescue: multichannel data collection and automation software is looking to help forward-thinking organizations first to define, then to locate, and finally to engage their ideal customers.

Email direct marketing campaign management is now only one part of marketing automation software capabilities.

Digital Marketing Depot's 2014 'Market Intelligence Report', called B2B Marketing Automation Tools 2014: A Marketer's Guide" cites eight key features that they say every major marketing automation software needs to deliver (http://digitalmarketingdepot.com/research_report/b2b-marketing-automation-tools-2013-the-marketers-guide?utm_source=sel&utm_medium=textlink&utm_campaign=buyersguide&utm_content=mir_1303_marketauto):

1. Dynamic content generation, including email campaigns and landing pages

2. Lead capturing, scoring, and nurturing

3. Scheduling and task management

4. Multichannel marketing, including social media and pay-per-click (PPC) and search engine optimization (SEO)

5. Multi-site and global support capabilities

6. Third-party app integration, including CRM (customer relationship management) systems and social applications

7. Budget tracking and forecasting

8. ROI analysis

Much of this software aims to close the gap, to give Marketing the analytics that it needs to form a high-definition picture of both the customers' engagement level throughout their journey and the activities of the sales reps. Marketing Automation (MA) technology is, of course, a response to the new breed of digital-age customers, but it also responds to many of the symptoms of Sales/Marketing misalignment that I discussed in Chapter 7.

While MA may have been a savior of sorts for organizations that suffered from ineffective communication or inefficient funnels or pipelines, I am, at best, cautiously optimistic when it comes to introducing automation into an organization that suffers from a lack of communication between Sales and Marketing, territorial disputes, or misaligned metrics.

Add to this the number of overlapping applications that organizations are using simultaneously and it becomes a very fuzzy picture indeed. Below is an illustration of this point. The image is courtesy of DNN and is the result of a <u>DNN survey</u> undertaken in 2014 that examined the number of marketing solutions that are in use in organizations of various sizes (<u>http://www.dnnsoftware.com/Portals/0/Whitepapers/DNN-2014-Research-Report-Marketing-Got-Complicated.pdf</u>).

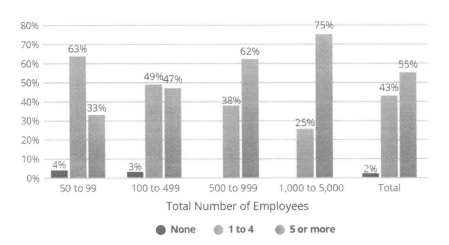

Number of Marketing Solutions
in Use by Company Size

Once again, I caution against viewing technology as some sort of magic bullet and don't mind repeating one of my favorite sayings here to reinforce the point:

"You can have the most sophisticated processes and the latest technology, but if your people are not with you then it will all come to nothing."

Accenture's report, called "Joining The Dots On Sales Performance" agrees with me (http://www.accenture.com/SiteCollectionDocuments/PDF/Accenture-Connecting-Dots-Sales-Performance.pdf).

Back in 2012 they said, *"The unvarnished truth is that a technology-centric approach has consistently failed to achieve results."*

According to the CSO Insights 2012 data, *"Fewer than 15% of organizations achieved improved win rates from implementing sales tools, mobile or otherwise.*

To make matters worse, more than 85% of surveyed organizations did not increase revenue from technology deployments, and more than 90% did not reduce the time it takes to close a sale."

This may not actually be a failure of the technology.

Recent data from Heinz Marketing and OnTarget Consulting and Research suggests that MA tools are paying the highest dividends 2-5 years *after* implementation (http://www.business2community.com/marketing-automation/marketing-automation-meeting-high-expectations-0866561#!IId1zc). Those companies enjoying successful implementation are the ones that are adopting a power-user model, which educates users to make the absolute most of the software's capabilities.

As ever, it is not the tool but the way that it is used that determines outcomes. Automating problematic processes, feeding automation software with incomplete, low-quality or outdated data, or increasing the audience for content without addressing the quality of that content will never produce a satisfying marketing ROI.

Almost one third of respondents to a 2014 B2B Online poll by Digital Marketing Depot, called 'B2B Marketing Automation Platforms 2014:

A Marketer's Guide', found poor Sales and Marketing alignment to be one of the most significant obstacles to effective marketing automation (http://www.marketo.com/reports/btob-research-insights-marketing-automation-best-practices-in-a-rapidly-changing-world/).

See the graphic below as a reference:

Budget constraints	32%
Poor integration betwwen sales and marketing	32%
Poor infrastructure to collect/analyze data	30%
LAck of lead data & support from sales	30%
Complexity of marketing automation software	23%
Inability to find trained employees	19%
Poor defined ROI	17%
Compatibility/interoperability issues	14%
Belief that current methods are ok	12%
Lack of performance standards	12%

Source: B2BOnline, Marketing Automation: Best Practices in a Rapidly Changing World

More effective training has the potential to increase marketing automation ROI, but as we'll see later, technology really only becomes effective when the human element and the right processes are first agreed on and set in place.

Chapter Takeaway

The world of marketing, like the world of sales, is almost unrecognizable from what it was as only a few decades ago. Online content marketing and social media channels, and the rich veins of buyers that can be reached through these new methods are forcing a re-evaluation of how marketing is to be conducted in the twenty-first century. To the delight of many marketers this includes a re-evaluation of marketing budgets, which have been trending upwards for some time and show no signs of reversing that trend.

Peter Strohkorb

Chapter 11:
Perceptions and Solutions

To produce the desired results, Sales+Marketing Collaboration has to take into account the department-specific trends that I outlined in the last two chapters. Customers, markets and technologies have all undergone varying degrees of upheaval in the last decade. Therefore, departmental grievances, particularly those between Sales and Marketing, must be addressed in ways that are mutually satisfactory. Each of these grievances is a hurdle to alignment, and a collaborative strategy that doesn't endeavor to clear these hurdles (by thoroughly addressing deep-seated grievances) is a fool's errand.

To help you get a good run-up to these hurdles, this chapter focuses on some of these grievances that would-be collaborators frequently encounter. After each observation, I have proposed a solution, invariably ones that has proven successful in my ongoing work to overcome the barriers to effective Sales+Marketing Collaboration.

Clearing these hurdles is absolutely essential if your end goal is the mutually beneficial partnership that inevitably follows in the wake of Sales+Marketing Collaboration.

We'll begin with the complaints that Sales usually addresses to Marketing. In the next section, Marketing will have its chance to return fire.

1. Sales' Perceptions

Sales Perception #1: Closing the loop between Sales and Marketing is a solution in and of itself.

There are dozens of automation tools that attempt to close the loop that connects Sales and Marketing, but automating arm's length processes rarely resolves tensions on its own. It seems to me that too many internal processes move in one direction only, namely from Marketing to Sales, and from there, on to suspects and prospects. Rarely is there an opportunity for Sales to provide constructive feedback to Marketing. This is problematic on several fronts: it makes Marketing feel that they are somehow superior to Sales; it makes Sales resent Marketing's tendency to pontificate and send the good word 'down from the mountain' to Sales.

One area in which improvements have been made is lead management. It used to be that Marketing would generate fresh sales leads, which would be handed to Sales (or at times just 'chucked over the fence') for follow-up. In today's more collaborative workplaces, Sales and Marketing try to agree on what actually constitutes a lead. This has led to new terminology that attempts to make the hand-off stage the site of ongoing dialogue between Sales and Marketing. Marketing Qualified Leads (MQLs) and Sales-Accepted Leads (SALs) usually reflect an agreed-upon quality standard that must be met before Sales accepts leads from Marketing. This has more closely defined both departments' responsibilities and made them more accountable.

Though this alone represents progress of a sort, a number of issues are still cropping up. Too often, Sales simply rejects a whole set of MQLs (often blaming Marketing for supposedly doing an inferior job). A feedback loop of sorts has been established, but it's being polluted by the same kinds of attitudes that made its establishment necessary in the first place. Even with these strategies in place, IDC still found that "only 25% of sales leads are used by sales teams". In other words, we're still not getting very far with this.

Proposed Solution:

Rather than rejecting large chunks of MQLs outright, Sales needs to be able to selectively pass them back to Marketing where they can be re-qualified or re-primed. Pounding on doors that are not ready to be opened or ones that are still locked up is what leads salespeople to operate independently of Marketing. Salespeople are not alchemists: they can not make gold from lead, so there does need to be some accountability on the part of Marketing that the leads that are being fed on to Sales are indeed properly qualified. Clear parameters as to what passes muster and what does not are important here. This can be as simple as quick follow up calls or texts between individual members, or it can be a part of regular Sales and Marketing alignment meetings.

Sales Perception #2: Marketing doesn't understand the ways in which sales are really produced. They are still acting under assumptions that are based on outdated business models.

Proposed Solution: Get Sales and Marketing on the same page by including both departments in joint planning meetings. Particular attention should be paid to the feedback that Sales has to offer regarding what Marketing collateral and initiatives really work to win deals. Whenever possible, give both departments joint sign-off powers on initiatives and have marketers shadow sales reps on their calls.

Sales Perception #3: Marketing doesn't properly listen to the feedback that Sales provides. It feels as though Sales and Marketing don't have shared objectives.

Proposed Solution: Without firm agreement on strategy, tactics and definitions, it's nearly impossible to engage Sales and Marketing in constructive dialogue, let alone find a winning formula. Brian Kardon, CMO at Lattice Engines, suggests the following questions as a starting point for the dialogue that needs to precede the much sought-after winning formula (http://www.lattice-engines.com/resources/ebooks/sales-marketing-alignment-guide):

- What is a Marketing-qualified lead?
- What is a Sales-accepted lead?
- What is a Sales-qualified opportunity?

Personally, I think it is unwise in the long term to have Marketing focus solely on sales lead generation and nurturing. After all, Marketing has a broader role to play in terms of brand positioning, brand profile, thought leadership, and differentiating the organization from its competitors. Still, Marketing needs to come to the table and work together with Sales to reach mutually agreeable definitions. This will not take minutes, hours, or even weeks. It's a process that will require both departments to divert no small amount of their energies and good will, but the sales productivity gain will more than make up for this initial investment of time and energy.

Kardon also suggests that once initial definitions are agreed upon, a second set of questions should be applied to the results:

- How many MQLs are being fed into the funnel?
- What is our conversion rate?
- How many opportunities are we creating?
- What is the resulting ROI?

Return to these questions until there is a workable agreement in place. Be wary of putting pegs in the ground before you've got concrete data that can show how subtle or major definition changes are affecting outcomes; a little bit of flexibility should be expected – or, if need be, demanded – of both sides.

Sales Perception #4: Marketing spends money without having anything to show for it. Without ever being accountable for revenue, Marketing spends what Sales earns.

Proposed Solution: Though it doesn't work for all organizations, some have chosen to tie Marketing's compensation to generated revenue. In order to be at all productive, this step should only be taken as part of a more broadly implemented collaborative strategy. In some cases, new compensation structures have engaged Marketing to provide better-qualified and nurtured leads and to proactively engage with the sales process in productive ways. You can expect pushback from Marketing should you decide to walk your organization down this path. If the strategy produces results, though, Marketing can see their share of the revenue pie rise substantially. The risk surrounding this strategy, however, is that it may well frustrate marketers as they may feel that they are being forced into a one-dimensional process, the success of which they have little control over.

2. Marketing's Perceptions

We've let Sales say its piece. Now it's Marketing's turn. What is crucial to remember is that, while many of these perceptions poorly reflect reality, none of them should be dismissed outright. In each of my proposed solutions, I suggest ways that collaborative strategies can be leveraged to deal with the roots of the problems. Ignoring negative feedback (no matter what the source) fosters resentment (and not just of the inter-departmental variety). Keep that in mind as you make your way through these perceptions and solutions.

Marketing Perception #1: Sales is the department that gets all the glory (and, more importantly, the financial incentives and rewards as well) for what is only the final stage in a long, labor-intensive and Marketing-initiated process.

Proposed Solution: Compensate Marketing for their role in the sales process. If they are lobbing softballs that Sales is knocking out of the park without breaking a sweat, there's no reason that Sales should hog all the credit (and the ensuing rewards). To the victor go the spoils, but an 'I touched it last' mentality only increases inter-departmental animosity. Allow this kind of attitude to put down roots and Marketing will start to question why they are putting in the extra effort to deliver purchase-ready leads to an ungrateful sales force.

At the same time, if they are to share in the rewards, there needs to be some accountability on the part of Marketing. Compensation and revenue should be related for marketers in ways that are similar (though not necessarily identical) to the ways in which they are related for salespeople. Bring Marketing into the loop in the sales process; give them reason to hound or support (as required) the salespeople who aren't closing business and less business will fall through the cracks.

Engaging Marketing in the sales process can, in many cases, make a sales force significantly more productive. I've seen empowered and interested marketing departments spur on dug-in salespeople with sloppy or inconsistent lead follow-up (these salespeople are often the ones who either rest on their laurels or meet expectations without ever exceeding them) by dramatically reducing or even cutting off their leads entirely. As ever, collaboration works best when it is a two-way street.

Marketing Perception #2: Sales is incompetent. The leads they are receiving from Marketing are well-qualified and primed, but the salespeople are unable or unwilling to engage with MQLs in a way that will result in a sale. They are squandering the good leads that Marketing is providing.

Proposed Solution: This is the volley most frequently returned from Marketing after they have endured wholesale criticism from Sales. Of course, it is nonsense. No salesperson would purposely avoid closing a sale that puts commission in their pocket just to spite Marketing.

I have found that focus on lead quality can distract from a larger issue that is often at the root of poor conversion rates: market prioritization. It is always worthwhile to ask which market segments are producing the highest ROI. After all, long buyer's journeys that consistently end in small purchases can conceal poor revenue behind high conversion rates. The size and number of conversions in a target market need to be weighed against the amount of sales pressure and the type and quality of the marketing collateral that is being applied in that market. If your fastest sales are emerging out of markets that are being under-targeted by either Sales or Marketing, then re-allocating resources to focus to those markets can dramatically influence the top and bottom lines. This is another important point for Marketing and Sales alignment: if Marketing is carpet-bombing markets that Sales is (for whatever reason) unable to penetrate, then it is crucial to re-evaluate which market segments and decision drivers Marketing has set its sights on.

Marketing Perception #3: Sales is lagging behind marketing strategies. They are comfortable selling the same products and services to which they are accustomed, or they have ideas of their own about what the customer wants, which means they are ignoring new products or services that represent the future of the organization.

Proposed Solution: This is a mindset issue, one that frequently leads to significant amounts of inter-departmental friction and to Sales developing its own collateral and generating their own leads. Leap this hurdle with the help of website analytics. It is mind-boggling that organizations that depend upon web traffic for a large portion of their sales are still reluctant to use the best available technologies to track the way that customers are engaging (or not) with their landing pages and other online materials. Heat maps can give you the data you need to act upon the ways in which customers are actually interacting with your site. You may be pushing your flagship product when it is interest in your entry-point product that is driving the majority of your website traffic. Rather than relying on customer surveys, which are notoriously unreliable, go straight to the source and see where Marketing and Sales need to focus their attention in unison. This kind of shift often means digging out entrenched salespeople, which is difficult to do unless you are armed with the kind of verifiable customer data that digital analytics can provide.

Marketing Perception #4: Sales is unreceptive to advice or feedback from Marketing. When approached individually, they are dismissive; when approached collectively, they are defensive. They come into meetings ready to shift blame, and the Sales Director tolerates, not to say encourages, this uncooperative behavior.

Proposed Solution: This is also a mindset issue: salespeople come to meetings with a handful of D.O.A. leads waiting for their 'gotcha' moment. Marketing is guilty of a similar practice, bringing a list of promising leads that were fed into the funnel or pipeline without tangible results, or even follow up. The finger pointing begins from the word go, and before long, the meetings are little more than grievance-airing sessions, ones that nobody – least of all middle management – looks forward to.

Jon Miller of Marketo says that when marketing and sales executives are able to come to agreement, this can often spur on their teams to do the same (http://www.lattice-engines.com/resources/ebooks/sales-marketing-alignment-guide). He suggests either a round of golf or a bucket of suds for the heads of marketing and sales departments. The culture is so often openly antagonistic that a *tête-a-tête* miles away from the office might do more good than a week's worth of meetings. This is not to say that a chummy extra-professional relationship between department heads will guarantee a more cooperative workplace, but the dialogue has to begin somewhere, and a corporate meeting room isn't always the right place. Keep this in mind, though: There is no guarantee that a night of collective imbibing will reset entrenched attitudes and beliefs. It usually takes far more than that to break down hardened barriers.

By the by, judicial use of specialist technology can help to make the bridging of this gap easier.

For example, I have been using an online app, called MeetingQuality, which helps me to make my own and my clients' meetings more productive. All it does is to send the meeting participants a very short 3-point evaluation form with an invitation to rate the other participants. After the meeting, each participant receives a report with the highest and the lowest score in the meeting as well as their own score for comparison purposes. All responses are anonymized so that feedback can be offered freely and without fear of reprisals. In my experience, the first time the tool is used most people dismiss their score. "What would the app know?" seems to be the prevailing attitude. However, people receiving a low score again after their second round of meeting evaluations show signs that they are starting to consider that the feedback might be valid and that they may have some room for improvement in regards to their meeting contribution quality. By the third meeting, everyone is trying harder to contribute productively and – *voila!* – meetings become more productive.

Frequency of Sales and Marketing Team Meetings

Never

Annually

Several times a year

3%

51%

More than once a week

10%

20%

17%

Weekly or fortnightly

Monthly

Successful

Unsuccessful

Another option is to adjust the frequency of formal meetings between sales and marketing teams.

My own research, comparing the Sales+Marketing Collaboration habits of growth organizations with their less successful counterparts, shows that the majority of financially successful organizations have their sales and marketing teams meet formally at least several times a year.

Also, there is, it seems, a tipping point between too little and too much structured contact between Sales and Marketing. Familiarity breeds contempt, but so too does estrangement. The balance to be struck is different for every organization. Make sure that, if you think more meetings will solve the issue, you are not inadvertently throwing more fuel on the fire. Experiment with meeting frequency until you find the right balance for your organization.

A final word before turning to some of the ways that organizations can go about encouraging a cooperative culture: celebrate victories, both small and large, together. This doesn't mean an end to department-specific recognition, but when effective cooperation between Sales and Marketing is clearly responsible for a successful campaign then make sure that both departments are recognized for their respective roles. If there are to be celebrations then try to facilitate dialogue between the departments and mutual backslapping by making sure that recognition is collective.

Chapter Takeaway

Even though – or perhaps because – it is increasingly difficult to delineate a hard and fast boundary between Sales and Marketing, the very pressures to perform that both teams find themselves constantly under continue to cause friction between these teams. This friction is best countered through quality teamwork as we are finding our way through the paradigm shift.

Chapter 12:
Portraits of Two Very Different Enterprizes

Let's briefly review the path we have travelled so far:

1) The fact that there is misalignment between Sales and Marketing departments is unavoidable. According to Richardson, a little fewer than 50% of sales teams understand their organization's content marketing strategy (http://www.richardson.com/PageFiles/Articles/content-marketing-sales-effectiveness-survey.pdf). In fact, almost a quarter of sales teams read nothing – or next to nothing – that Marketing produces. Many poorly aligned organizations are characterized by disconnects such as these. Since approximately two thirds of customers are looking for a customer experience that is seamless, integrated, and consistent – which is as rare as hen's teeth when the left hand doesn't know what the right is doing – the importance of getting these two departments on the same page is more important than ever. Mountains of research show that sales teams are skeptical when it comes to the content that their marketing partners are producing; there is a crisis of confidence with – again, as per

Richardson – nearly 50% of sales professionals reporting that they have little or no faith in the content that is produced by Marketing. Each department is skeptical of the other's contributions, but this skepticism is often founded upon misconceptions, stereotypes, and poor communication. Fingers point across the aisle: Marketing says that Sales incompetence is at the root of poor performance; Sales says that Marketing's useless content and leads are the problem, and the prevalent siloed approach merely entrenches such positions.

2) The old sales funnel is dying and the Buyer's Journey is upon us, which means that the way organizations attract interest and hawk their wares is changing dramatically. Endowed with information streams and technology tools like never before, customers are increasingly demanding a more sophisticated, information-rich and advisory approach from sales reps. This is having untold effects. Some well-positioned organizations with established brands, products and knowledgeable salespeople have found buyers who are already purchase-ready at initial touch points. For emerging or struggling organizations whose reputation is still being established, buyer's journeys are stretching interminably, stuck for eternities in the dreaded 'do nothing' or 'wait and see' stages. Whether emerging or established, organizations that are not adjusting to the new paradigm are likely to go the way of the dinosaur.

3) While it is by no means the only barrier to partnership, the largest hurdle to clear in terms of Sales+Marketing Collaboration is located where the two functions intersect: at the entrance to the pipeline. Sales most frequent complaint is that Marketing doesn't produce the high-quality leads that they need in order to sell. Marketing insists that their job is to generate general interest in their business offerings, not to qualify leads.

4) As previously mentioned, this can lead to a huge gulf in the perception of what actually constitutes a sales lead. Here is the crux: Marketing may consider a name and a phone number a sales lead, whereas sales reps ideally may want a customer with a purchase order at the ready, together with the accompanying payment. In a bizarre twist, in my experience lead generation initiatives are usually led by Marketing and the nurturing of these leads is often simply imposed on Sales without any substantial input or consultation. Without mutually agreed-upon definitions and metrics in place, leads will be frittered away through inefficient pipelines. What is desperately needed is something that improves the quality and the consistency of Sales' feedback, i.e. a structured, measurable and, most importantly, constructive way for Sales to inform Marketing what works and what doesn't and, crucially, why. We need to close the feedback loop back from Sales to Marketing and to create a virtuous cycle of collaboration that stops wasting time, money and effort on both sides and allows both teams to live up to their full potential.

5) The costs of misalignment and poor communication between Sales and Marketing are substantial. Today's buyers demand a consistent experience across all touch points, and, since bad experiences can have as much viral potential as good ones, misalignment can manifest itself in a wide range of symptoms:

- Diminished brand value
- Missed revenue targets
- Reduced agility and market responsiveness
- High staff churn
- Long or interminable buyer's journeys or sales cycles

- Inaccurate sales forecasts
- Ineffective marketing spend
- Uncontrolled discounting by sales reps

According to a 2011 IDC report as cited by Amanda F. Batista, misalignment is directly responsible for upwards of 10% of revenue loss each year. Industry experts have frequently cited this figure, warning of the bottom-line impact that the siloed approach is having, particularly on larger B2B organizations.

My own research shows that organizations that are forward-thinking in terms of Sales+Marketing Collaboration are being rewarded for anticipating the bend in the road:

54.5% of companies that reported revenue growth have a combined Sales+Marketing department.

54,5%

54.5% of companies that reported revenue growth have a combined Sales/Marketing department.

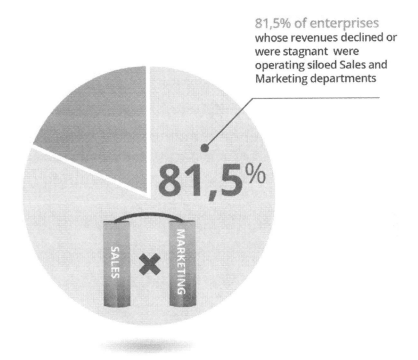

81,5% of enterprises whose revenues declined or were stagnant were operating siloed Sales and Marketing departments

Not convinced?

Take a look at the other side of the coin: 81.5% of enterprizes in our test group whose revenues declined or were stagnant were operating across siloed Sales and Marketing departments.

With these important points in mind, let's explore what collaborative enterprize actually looks like.

The following are two entirely hypothetical examples, let's call them *Silo Inc.* and *Team Corp.* Though they are both fictional, some of the eye-popping details are taken from organizations and their sales and marketing departments that I have personally encountered in my research and in my work as a consultant.

As the following points will make clear, too many of today's B2B organizations have approached the issue of collaboration in general and the Sales vs. Marketing question in particular in ways that leave much to be desired.

Silo Inc.: An Example Of Poor Sales+Marketing Collaboration

- A global B2B powerhouse through much of the '80s and '90s, Silo Inc. has watched its revenue steadily decline since 2001. This decline accelerated sharply after the GFC in 2008 and then again with the advent of a disruptive new competitor in 2011.

- Silo Inc.'s Australian headquarters occupies a six-floor commercial building in Sydney's equivalent to Silicon Valley. The reception area and the warehouse are on the ground floor; Customer Service is on the second floor; Sales is on the third and fourth floors; Marketing and Customer Service are on the fifth floor; and HR, Legal, Corporate Operations and the senior executives are all on the top floor. The CEO has his own enormous corner office with sweeping views of the city.

- The CIO has been convinced by technology vendors that automation is the solution to all the organization's problems and that by eliminate these problems he will raise his personal profile both inside and outside of his employer organization.

- A business case was drawn up by a mid-tier executive team and approved by the Executive Committee.

- Silo Inc. has thus invested millions in wide-ranging CRM, MA, SE, and SFA software.

- No two people in the office use these systems in the same way, and there is considerable resistance from end users. They feel that they were not properly consulted and that this new system was forced upon them.

- There is a distinct 'us vs. them' attitude present in almost all of the interactions between departments. Inter-departmental communication is rife with condescension, sarcasm, disrespect, and barely concealed contempt.

- Senior staff members each have their own closed-door offices.

- Marketing and Sales each have separate meeting rooms on different floors. When entering the other's floor, there is a distinct feeling that one is in somebody else's 'turf'. Neither side does anything to combat this feeling, using seating arrangement and fraternalism to remind inter-departmental visitors that they are indeed outsiders.

- There are a number of satellite offices, each of which is similarly structured. However, as there are no regional marketing people the attitude is not just 'us vs. them' in relation to Sales and Marketing but 'us vs. them' in relation to anything that comes from the regional head office in Sydney.

- Each and every location, be it in Australia, India, China, the Middle East or the U.K., receives identical brochures and other collateral from the overseas head office in Asia. In the name of corporate consistency, all locations are told to use these materials without fail (they have, after all, been tested extensively). The translations are stilted and free of nuance; if the mother tongue is English, the collateral is identical in every way to the material used in the American offices.

- One particularly obviously global HQ-designed brochure features on its front page a stereotypical representation of ethnic groups that are not represented in the local Australian community.

- There is the equivalent of a barbed-wire fence between both the local and the overseas' head office Sales and Marketing functions. MQLs are thrown over the fence, but there is no transparency, so there is inconsistent (frequently non-existent) follow-up on the part of sales. Sales frequently throws leads back over the fence (or into the waste bin), but rarely offers detailed reasons for doing so.

- When Marketing confronts Sales about wasted leads, Sales (especially the indirect sales force) responds with, "I only want leads where the customer is ready to buy right now."

- Marketing has a MQL quantity quota, which they meet consistently.

- Sales frequently complains that the leads being 'thrown over the fence' are practically 'useless'.

- Marketing says that there's nothing wrong with the leads; the problem, they say, is that the sellers are lazy, incompetent and unappreciative.

- To meet their sales quotas, salespeople are drumming up their own leads, any way they can, including creating their own Marketing collateral and 'ghost products'.

- There is substantial animosity between Sales and Marketing. It's not infrequent for salespeople to say that "only real men have sales targets," while marketers refer to salespeople as "cavemen" or "knuckle-draggers".

- At corporate functions, the two groups never mingle, and at last year's Christmas party, there was one particularly non-festive interaction between a salesman and a marketer who had recently come to loggerheads over MQLs.

- There are quarterly review meetings with the heads of Sales and Marketing and other departments' senior executives attending. While junior sales reps and marketers engage in frequent finger pointing and chest thumping each department is quick to assign blame, yet slow to accept any. The heads of Sales and Marketing in these meetings prefer to pretend that all is well between their teams and that there are no problems with collaboration to speak of. They believe that as senior leaders they could be personally held responsible by the upper echelons of executives for the lack of team play. After all, who wants to risk making a career-limiting move by admitting fault? Thus, the senior executive team remains blissfully unaware of the real depth of conflict between the Sales and Marketing departments.

- In 2013, a new Marketing Director came and made his first order of business a corporate re-branding project. He presented the idea and what it could mean for the organization enthusiastically, citing nearly a dozen examples of vertical market competitors who had seen substantial ROI after implementing similar programs. He commissioned an external branding specialist to redesign Silo Inc.'s logo, style guide and mission statement, together with website re-design, a new multi-channel media strategy and the appointment of a new advertising and corporate communications agency. He had his marketing team meet with him on this project frequently, going through a number of different options before deciding on the new brand package that bore almost no resemblance to the older, already established logo.

- As the re-branding exercise was considered confidential, only the head of each department was informed but not allowed to pass this information on further.

- While this rebranding was still in its initial stages, the new Marketing Director also ran an initiative that was designed to help transform the organization from product-focus to customer-focus. Marketing spent weeks designing and refining a mind map to illustrate the various aspects of the new customer, their expectations, and their needs and demands, all in contrast to the current state of affairs.

- One floor down, Sales was just celebrating a pair of recent successes. After a raft of positive product reviews in an industry publication, two C-suite buyers in prospect organizations, both of whom had been stalled at the 'do nothing' stage for ages, had finally agreed to make substantial purchases.

- The Marketing Director called a meeting in order to discuss the rebranding project and the new customer-centric approach. As they entered the room, salespeople could be heard snickering at the mind map and a number of them referred to it during the meeting as the "sperm chart". When one senior marketer insisted that a rebranded, customer-centric organization would open doors that were previously closed to salespeople, a sales manager shifted the focus to the recent sales win, surprisingly subtly reminding the senior marketer that it was ultimately deals like that one that paid his salary.

- Enthusiasm surrounding Marketing's strategies waned after the meeting and the new logo's rollout was lackluster to say the least. Some salespeople continued to use collateral that featured the old logo.

- Before the end of the year, the two top-performing salespeople had moved on to greener pastures, the new Marketing Director had been replaced, and the most promising of the recent marketing hires had taken his talents to a local start-up.

- Nothing had changed in return for all that time, effort and money that the organization invested.

Now, let's explore what the alternative looks like.

'Team Corp': An Example of Good Sales +Marketing Collaboration

- A relative newcomer, Team Corp was incorporated in 1995. They met with early success due to a massively popular product offering that seemed prescient in terms of the coming mobile revolution.

- When revenues dipped in 2008, Team Corp responded proactively, adjusting their collateral and their means of communicating and engaging with their customers.

- They also rolled out a new range of budget-conscious products that proved to be very much in line with what customers were looking for during the economic downturn. As the economy recovered, so too did the sales of their flagship product.

- When it became clear that their systems and procedures were in danger of falling behind the curve, the Team Corp executives agreed to pursue automation, albeit cautiously.

- The CMO in consultation with the CIO and a range of vendors very quickly realized that technology would only take them so far and that teamwork was going to be the key to their future success.

- The CMO embarked on a collaboration program and was lauded by the CEO for his pro-active initiative. That prize was all that was needed to also bring the Sales Director on board.

- An executive team was established to consult widely, particularly among the end user community and ended up selecting the most suitable (not the lowest cost) vendor.

- The first six months with the new CRM, MA, and SE systems saw very little ROI, so they adopted a collaboration methodology that specifically included the end users (i.e. not just management), and investing heavily in joint end user workshops and inter-team coaching.

- A year later, everybody within the organization had aligned to hone operations and procedures into a fine point.

- After a record-breaking year in 2011, Team Corp decided to move into new, more collaborative workspaces. Beginning with their London headquarters, they engaged a consulting firm on workspace productivity and focused on encouraging impromptu discussions and meetings between teams of different competencies.

- The office was featured in a number of industry and design magazines, and it wasn't long before all the offices around the world were given the green light to follow suit.

- The new arrangement brought Sales and Marketing into closer contact with each other, and while, at first, there were some frictions, management instituted a monthly Sales and Marketing meeting. Early on, these meetings were grievance sessions.

- A neutral, third-party 'referee' was brought in to help facilitate communication. Within three months, the meetings were about aligning strategy, tactics and procedures to drive the success of all parties involved.

- Within another three months, the neutral third party was no longer required at the meetings. Grievances were addressed in separate channels, and the meetings were limited to information-sharing and decision-making: Sales had customer feedback to share and Marketing had new research, content, and resources to discuss.

- The corporate head office in London relaxed the style guide and guidelines in terms of how Marketing was to produce collateral and how Sales was to use it (demanding, for instance, that color palette and font remain the same regardless of region but allowing for more nuanced messages that respond more sensitively to the local community, its requirements and its expectations).

- In each campaign and every piece of collateral, there is a balancing of the head office macro and the regional micro message.

- There is no longer an obvious barrier between Sales and Marketing. Feedback from front-line salespeople is valued and promptly responded to by Marketing. There are no negative sentiments if Sales finds a lead-generation technique or a specific piece of Marketing collateral ineffective. It can go back to Marketing and expect the matter to be rectified without fuss.

- Though Sales and Marketing remain different departments, they now have a common understanding of each other's roles and carry shared KPIs. When Sales has an exceptional quarter, Marketing is also recognized and to a degree compensated for their role in that success.

- Marketing is thus judged not by the quantity of their lead generation or appointments but by sales outcomes. Sales is, in part, evaluated according to opening ratios and the quality of the feedback it provides to Marketing. Doing so increased MQL closure by 23%, SQL closure by 12%, revenue from Marketing leads by 16%, and drove up key account retention by 18% (similar numbers are reported in a 2013 MathMarketing and Marketo report on Sales and Marketing alignment).

- Overall, there is an understanding between the departments that success is not individual or departmental: it is collective. This philosophy is now starting to extend to customer service, warehouse, and human resources functions as well.

- When a time-strapped customer showed up early for a meeting with a sales rep (who was busy with another client at that time), a quick-thinking Marketer was able to walk the customer through the sales presentation, which she had helped the sales rep to prepare. The sales rep, entering the boardroom near the end of the presentation, allowed the Marketer to finish the presentation without interrupting. When the presentation was over, the customer, impressed with both the presentation and the quality of collaboration was happy to extend his contract. Tellingly, he happily accepted a request for a written testimonial.

- There is a forum on the Team Corp's intranet, on which employees ask questions and offer advice. Though few people used it at first, within six months, it became a place in which the organization could engage employees in a global dialogue. No matter what time zone you were in and no matter what time a question was put up on the forum, somebody would address the question or their suggestion on how to resolve the issue within 24 hours, and often faster than that.

- As the company continued to grow, executives focused their energies on keeping the operational teams relatively small. These small collaborative pockets mimic small businesses, preserving the entrepreneurial spirit within a large corporate governance framework. By keeping the team size small, they also created an environment in which most people knew each other at a personal level. This in turn motivated everyone be the best that they could be and to help each other achieve their personal and collective goals.

- Staff turnover rates have shrunk to historical lows. Whenever there is a vacancy at this organization, they find themselves in the enviable position of being able to select from a large number of highly qualified and eager applicants (word had spread around that Team Corp supports, engages, and rewards its employees and that it is the place to work for those who want to make their mark in the industry).

Chapter Takeaway

As the two (only marginally hypothetical) examples above demonstrate, effective collaboration positive impacts a large number of parameters, be they financial, cultural, tangible or intangible. Collaborative organizations are happier and more successful places where people want to build careers.

Peter Strohkorb

Chapter 13:
The 7 Common Mistakes of Would-Be Collaborators

Look before you leap. While Sales+Marketing Collaboration can dramatically improve both functions in an organization, as we saw in the Silo Inc. and Team Corp examples above, there is a right way and a wrong way to implement and facilitate true collaboration. Knowing where the opportunities and threats are makes the job all the easier, so let's look at the places where would-be collaborators most frequently founder.

1. Doing Nothing

We discussed this early on, but it's a point that bears repeating. The worst mistake one can make is to turn a blind eye to problems. Denying that there is room for improvement or merely accepting the *status quo* can magnify issues that would be otherwise manageable. In far too many companies, sales and marketing departments are working in their respective silos, largely unaware of, or ill-equipped for, the changing world that surrounds them. Too many organizations have taken this path and suffered for it. How did Kodak miss the digital-camera revolution? How did Canon not see the threat from smartphones with in-built cameras?

Doing nothing is a very risky strategy.

At perhaps a more tactical level, this problem manifests itself when sales reps using twentieth-century selling techniques are unable to get their foot in the door with their twenty-first-century customers. The new buyer expects reps to approach them well prepared and with a complete understanding of their problems; they want added value and subject-matter expertise; they want content, not pitches. Anything less than suitable and sustainable solutions that respond to their specific needs and they'll start to look towards the competition. In order to address this demanding customer, the rep and the organization as a whole must both recognize that the customer and their buying process is no longer what he once was. This is a problem that must be overcome, and sitting on our hands will get us nowhere, really fast.

2.   Believing that Technology will deliver a Miracle

There are many vendors out there that come with their latest whizz-bang technology in hand, promising the world. Most organizations have already implemented CRMs, but, according to Forrester's report, 'Answers To Five Frequently Asked Questions About CRM Projects', more than 47% of CRM projects fail at some level.

My personal experience is that reps don't like spending their time inputting data that reports their activities to management unless they feel that this process is somehow moving sales forward. Sales Enablement (SE) technology is different in this regard, provided it is implemented in the right way. Rather than feeling that they are giving something up (be it time or information) sales reps can see pretty quickly whether or not they are receiving something in return for their efforts. Having said that, technology can make well-oiled systems run better, but it will rarely increase productivity if the processes that it is applied to are bad to begin with, e.g. data quality and the underlying processes need to be relatively airtight for technology to be effective.

My own research shows that technology can be a powerful tool that is crucial to B2B sales success, but it seems that there can be such a thing as too much technology.

62% of the businesses I surveyed that were using CRMs as their only sales-supporting IT system saw their revenues decline. At the other end of the spectrum, running the technology gamut, i.e. implementing *three or more* of the following IT solutions: CRM, SE, SFA, and MA, made things much, much worse.

Have a look at the graphic below:

Only 8% of organizations that were technology-saturated in this way managed to grow their revenues. The best performers were those who travelled in the 'Goldilocks Zone' between too little and too much technology. 88% of those who implemented a combination of CRM and Sales Enablement (SE) technologies experienced revenue growth. This strategy far outstrips all the other combinations.

The most technologically advanced companies are not, it seems, necessarily the most profitable ones.

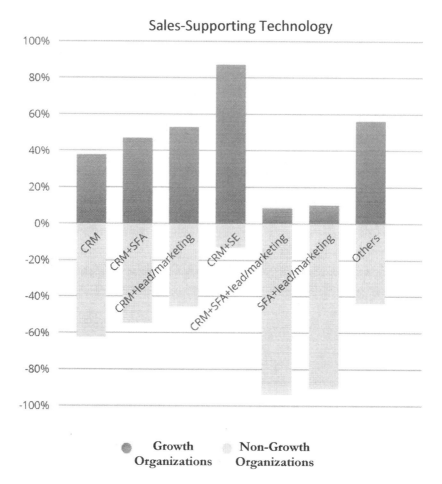

As a customer-facing tool, technology extends and amplifies reach and message, but beyond a certain tipping point, it can set the customer's teeth on edge. A wealth of customer research shows that, while automation may be effective in terms of providing qualified leads, the qualification process, when automated, can alienate more potential customers than it qualifies.

A recent <u>Sales Benchmark Index marketing automation report</u> warns against putting too much faith in the automation process (<u>http://www.salesbenchmarkindex.com/blog/3-root-causes-of-marketing-automation-failure-and-how-to-fix-them</u>): "Buyers who are early or midway through the buying process don't want to be 'qualified'. They want to engage and discuss key concepts." Still, 80% of those in the market for automation software are, according to <u>Besondy</u>, expecting this software to nurture their leads for them. To me, this is the automating the wrong processes. Automation should facilitate, but never replace, contact between customers and Vendors (<u>http://www.besondyllc.com/marketing-automation-trends/</u>).

As a tool for producing internal efficiencies, technology is still lagging behind expectations. <u>Jim Dickie of *CRM Magazine*</u> recently noted that, after a decade-long rise in the percentages of organizations leveraging CRMs, last year, for the first time, analysts "witnessed a drop in the percentage of salespeople who actively use CRM solutions as part of their daily workflow." (<u>http://www.destinationcrm.com/Articles/Columns-Departments/Reality-Check/The-Adoption-Rate-Challenge-94828.aspx?ll_p=9813e609-2586-44f6-8d8e-c1c8dc25cb0c&ll_e=pstrohkorb@ps-consulting.com.au&ll_c=14225&ll_mi=32301&ll_j=25842</u>).

While the numbers of organizations investing in CRMs continues to rise, those who are using the technology seem to have reached a saturation point. This is largely due to the mistaken focus on the technology's capabilities and not the user's. It is pretty obvious that even the most sophisticated technology will remain ineffective if you don't have your people and your business processes aligned first. Just because software *can* do something does not mean that you need it to. In other words, you don't need to use all the features and functions that software offers, just the ones that actually generate a business benefits and that the organization can cope with from a change management perspective.

Organizations that try to implement too much technology can very easily end up with very little business.

The core problem is not with the under-utilized technology, it is with the sales force's resistance to automation. When I have broached the topic of CRMs with salespeople, their complaints about the technology have been consistent: CRMs are, they feel, more a sales management and surveillance tool than a sales-support apparatus.

Salespeople are reluctant to give up their autonomy without anything in exchange, and that is precisely what they *are* being asked to do. What they feel is their personal IP – prospect/customer contacts, relationships and interactions – is being scrutinized in ever-increasing ways, and they feel like they're being hit with a double whammy: they're handing over highly valuable knowledge and they're being micro-managed more tightly. The question that keeps on coming up in interviews with salespeople is "What's in it for me?" If you can't answer that question, you'll want to take a closer look at the OneTEAM Trinity, which we'll discuss in detail in Chapter 18.

3. Implementing 'Band-Aid' Solutions

The world is increasingly impatient, and so are we; our attention spans are getting shorter, so it is no wonder that, when problems arise, we look for quick fixes. Shortcuts and roundabouts rarely work when it comes to Sales+Marketing Collaboration. When reps do not make their targets, many organizations try to address the problem with one or all of the following three short-term, 'quick fix' solutions.

Let's look at each of them in turn:

Hiring More Reps

The rationale for this popular choice is as follows: if X number of reps brings in Y amount of revenue, then increasing X will increase Y as well. However, hiring new sales reps is not a step that one should take lightly.

There is considerable risk and cost associated with the hiring process. According to Aberdeen Group, the average cost of onboarding new sales staff is US$29,060 per employee. An average of 6.24 man-months is spent on hiring and training (http://www.aberdeen.com/Aberdeen-Library/8787/RA-sales-performance-management.aspx).

That is the cost *before the rep even puts his or her feet under their desk*!

Simply adding more staff is rarely the solution to poor sales performance. On the contrary, adding new staff without addressing the underlying issues that are at the heart of poor sales performance is the equivalent trying to break up a brawl between cats and dogs merely by adding one more dog to the mix.

Applying More Training

This is a very popular quick fix. It has the advantage of ticking the 'completed' box for many sales managers who carry sales training or up-skilling as part of their job deliverables. Most sales managers rarely attend or even participate in this sales training, though. Instead, they send their reps on a two- or three-day sales training course and, as if through magic, expect them to come back enlightened, motivated, and cooperative. Managers might expect their reps to be as enthusiastic about the training as they are, but since the reps' sales targets are rarely adjusted to compensate for the lost selling time, they may feel as though training is more hindrance than help. For those who are really struggling to meet their targets, training courses can feel like an outright punishment.

According to the nineteenth-century German psychologist Hermann Ebbinghaus, 87% of new knowledge is forgotten within 30 days (http://en.wikipedia.org/wiki/Hermann_Ebbinghaus) . What do you think happens 30 days after the sales training? Most of this training comes with little to no post-training follow up. The sales training often ends with a meek "send us an email if you have any more questions," which is hardly useful when the sales rep is standing in front of a customer or on a deadline to finish a sales proposal.

Perhaps I'm being a little uncharitable to sales trainers when I say that I am not aware one of very many formal sales training programs that insist on making the ongoing coaching of individual reps compulsory, after the initial sales training days are finished. In my opinion, it is neither fair nor realistic to expect anyone to execute a new method immediately (let alone successfully) after the learning experience without some degree of follow-up that nurtures them up their personal learning curves. 'Set and forget' does not work in sales training.

Producing More Leads

More leads is another sure-fire way to boost sales results, right? Well, it would be if all your sales lead creation and management processes were perfect, i.e. if Sales and Marketing were working harmoniously together to generate, nurture, hand over, close and report on leads perfectly. If that is not the case, why would you want to spend good money creating more leads, only to see them lead nowhere thanks to a flawed process? Increasing MQL quotas only has a positive effect when Sales is suffering from a lack of leads. If it is the quality of the leads or, more frequently, the misaligned Sales and Marketing process that is driving poor sales numbers then stuffing more leads into a flawed funnel or pipeline will rarely achieve the hoped-for results. More does not automatically equal better.

4. There is no dedicated Person or Team responsible for improving Sales and Marketing Collaboration

Sales and Marketing obviously need to work together. For such cooperation to be possible, cross-functional processes need to be in place to make sure that both sides are in alignment. So, who is responsible for reaching across the aisle? Is it up to Marketing to work together with Sales, or is it vice versa? What happens when they can't come together on their own initiative?

The best way to achieve success is to have a dedicated but neutral third party in place whose job it is to ensure that the collaboration between Sales and Marketing is implemented and maintained. They can get the dialogue started so that both sides can agree on what processes and metrics will be applied moving forward. This mediated dialogue can often defuse any burgeoning issues before they escalate. Before any kind of cooperation can begin, it is important that all parties agree on the process steps, the definitions and the underlying metrics, otherwise communication issues – latent or blatant ones – will merely exacerbate the situation. Get a referee.

5. Neglecting the Human Element

When attempting to foster a cooperative relationship between Sales and Marketing, it is important to address the human dimension immediately. Few things are as powerful as the realization that, more often than not, everybody within an organization is purpose aligned – we are all pulling at the same rope, all trying to achieve the same outcome. When Sales and Marketing are at loggerheads, it is easy for both sides to forget this. Sales and Marketing need to understand and agree on *what* their roles actually are and how those roles relate to other roles within the organization. Only then will it be appropriate to move on to *how* each department can support the other; only then can we move on to the nuts and bolts of setting up joint processes and shared metrics.

An important aspect of addressing the human element is remembering that there is often a substantial difference between facts and perceptions. The language gap between Sales and Marketing is proof positive of this. Each department is assured that they are being understood, but closer analysis doesn't bear this out. I have frequently encountered this phenomenon in my research: more often than not there is a wide gap between Sales and Marketing in terms of each department's responses to questions designed to gauge their department's collaborative contributions. Sales thinks it's being clear and is being understood by Marketing and vice versa, but ask each department if they understand the other and the gap between perception and reality comes into sharp focus. Egos and interests can keep even the best-intentioned professionals from seeing the forest for the trees.

Sales vs. Marketing: Perceived levels of Collaboration

The graphs here are from our 2014 research report and highlight nicely just how wide a perception gap there can be between Sales and Marketing. We asked sales and marketing people separately about fourteen specific collaborative processes and whether they thought these exist in their organizations, or not. The rather fascinating results are illustrated below.

Now, how to interpret the graphs?

In a highly collaborative office, the gray and orange lines would meet in the middle (at the equal 50% mark). The more collaborative organizations are the ones in which there is more widespread agreement between Sales and Marketing in almost every category (i.e. the ones where the gray ad orange lines meet closer to the center).

Not only are the growth organizations better aligned, they are more profitable as well.

This means that there is now a clear and direct correlation between Sales+Marketing Collaboration and business success.

You can find the latest version of this research report on our website.

Growth Organisations

Non-Growth Organisations

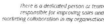

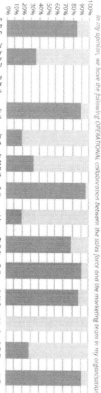

There is a dedicated person or team responsible for improving sales and marketing collaboration in my organisation

Marketing has a good understanding of what marketing material is being used by the high performing sales people, and how it is used

Marketing and sales are well aligned through shared objectives and joint performance metrics

Marketing has good understanding of the sales objectives

Sales has a good understanding of Marketing's objectives

Marketing consults with sales in the creation and management of marketing collateral and sales lead generation campaigns

Sales consults with Marketing prior to setting sales targets

Marketing has insight to the sales forecast, always / often / sometimes / rarely / never

Sales has input into the creation and improvement of marketing collateral, both online and offline

Sales has input into the planning and into the outcome of marketing campaigns

Both sales and marketing have access to the sales pipeline and related account information

There is a formal process for capturing, creating and distribution of customer testimonials

There is a central digital repository for the sales force to access all relevant sales and marketing material

It is easy for the sales force to find specific marketing collateral

● **Marketing Perspective**
○ **Sales Perspective**

● **Marketing Perspective**
○ **Sales Perspective**

Your marketing messaging and your sales messaging really should be aligned so as to speak with a single voice and not to confuse the buyer when they move from the research phase in the Buyer's Journey to contacting your sales rep. Having just returned from a Sales and Marketing Alignment conference in Chicago, USA, I can tell you that everybody there offered one 'point solution' or another on that theme. The messages have been familiar for some time now: "just use our sales training," "just adopt our marketing messaging system," "just get our leadership coaching program," and of course "just deploy our software". This is what I call 'point solutions', i.e. ones that resolve only a small part of an issue without addressing the underlying, broader causes.

These would-be collaborators are missing the forest for the trees. Since nobody is pulling all of the collaboration aspects together, success is short-lived at best, and elusive at worst. Though there was plenty of discussion focused on process alignment – especially when technology could be deployed in the name of that alignment – there was no mention at the conference of *people* working together. This is what makes the OneTEAM Method™ different and this is what makes it so timely.

Collaboration can be a deeply inter-personal matter: it relies on people doing the right thing by each other. No number of point solutions can bring people together like true collaboration can. This is why the OneTEAM Method™ starts with the *people* dimension. Only once the people within an organization are ready, and willing, to collaborate will point solutions fall on truly fertile ground. The people need to come first.

6. Trying to implement Change without Executive Buy-in

When change touches on aspects of corporate culture, implementing reforms can be an uphill battle (and a steep one at that). As laudable as it might be for middle managers or junior staff to attempt to make cultural changes, such optimistic projects are often doomed to failure unless they have executive buy-in.

According to <u>Aberdeen Group</u>, 86% of world-leading organizations have buy-in at the highest levels in terms of their sales performance management, whereas only 56% of underperformers can claim the same   (http://www.aberdeen.com/Aberdeen-Library/8787/RA-sales-performance-management.aspx).

This doesn't mean that change has to come solely from the top, but there does need to be a chorus of nodding heads all the way up the ladder.

Remember, senior executives are time poor; they like low-risk, fact-driven initiatives. The key to getting senior executives on board is to present them with a compelling business case that is rich with value-based data to back up the arguments in favor of the proposed change. Get the boss involved.

7. Expecting immediate Results

Too often, we expect overnight results, and sometimes even that's not fast enough. The fact is, any change must be given time to work its way through the system if it is to have any chance to produce positive outcomes. There very well may be a quick wins that can be realized in the short term, but the bigger wins almost always take time. Don't expect or demand anything to happen overnight. Technology implementation, like metric or process adjustments, can take longer than you think to have a tangible, bottom-line impact.

"Y'all just get along now, all right?"

As we have all learned at some point or another, patience pays dividends. Sales+Marketing Collaboration, when done right, is not as simple as plugging in a new device or as flicking a switch. It will produce the kind of results that will make the investment more than worthwhile, but only if it is given time to work its way through all three levels of the OneTEAM™ Productivity Trinity, which we will be turning to shortly.

Chapter Takeaway

The seven mistakes above are surprisingly widespread in many organizations that I encounter. It strikes me that avoiding them would be a relatively simple matter if would-be collaborators knew what to look for, what to expect, and what to avoid. Even before that, though, must come the penny-dropping realization that something is amiss and that something must be done to address the problem.

That is why I put 'Doing Nothing' at the top of my list of mistakes.

Chapter 14:
Why I Developed the OneTEAM Method™

So far, I have described the issues that today's sales and marketing teams are facing. I have also offered a number of strategies that focus on specific collaborative issues. It is time to tell you how and why I came to develop the OneTEAM Method™.

It didn't happen overnight. It is the fruit of over 15 years of personal experience working in both sales and marketing roles for some of the largest B2B brands on the planet. The observations that I made over those years all led me to the same conclusion: We are in the midst of a collaborative crisis.

I watched carefully, noticing what strategies worked and which ones didn't. As I began to develop a coherent theory surrounding collaboration, these observations were tempered with third-party research from some of the finest specialist firms in the world. To this I added academic research findings taken from all corners of the developed world. Finally, I conducted my own research in search of new answers, asking questions third-party researchers and academics had largely ignored. Though this book represents something of a focal point in this journey, my learning continues unabated. Each year, I update my research findings. You can find my latest 30-odd page research report on the peterstrohkorbconsulting.com website, where it is available free of charge.

The OneTEAM Method™ was developed because I experienced first-hand the frustration that abounds on both sides when Sales and Marketing do not cooperate effectively. I have seen good people in Marketing spend valuable time, effort and money to produce content and leads for the sales team, only to see them not being used. On the other side, I have heard salespeople say that Marketing is not supporting them and then come to the conclusion that they need to do their own marketing, with all the negative consequences that this entails in terms of lost time, opportunity and messaging consistency. Thus, I have seen and experienced the frustration that results from wasted time, effort and money on both sides.

The crux of the problem is that the longer this disconnect continues, the further apart it drives each department from the other. They retreat deeper and deeper into their silos, behaving like jilted lovers, eventually shutting each other out completely.

And, just like it is with jilted lovers, the disconnect almost inevitably becomes personal. Over the years, I have witnessed some downright nasty comments being lobbed back and forth. To illustrate this, here are some low-lights:

A mid-ranking sales manager in a global technology vendor organization, pulling a face like he had just bitten into a lemon, had this to say about Marketing: "What would they know? Real men carry sales targets." The implication – not difficult to detect – is that Marketing is full of sissies with scant understanding of the 'real world' that sales reps inhabit. He went on to suggest that marketers cower behind their jargon, concealing their arrogance behind talk about segmentation, targeting and positioning, etc.

Marketers are no more charitable than salespeople when they speak about reps. One senior marketing leader in a mid-sized consulting firm had this to say about her own organization's sales force: "What is the difference between a sales rep and a marketer?" She paused for effect, and then answered her own question: "An education!" Ouch! Talk about a cheap shot.

Her delivery suggested that she'd used this nugget before. She seemed surprised when I didn't laugh, probably because she is used to delivering the joke among her peers, many of whom might share her thinly-veiled belief that sales reps are all uneducated knuckle-draggers who don't even have the capacity to appreciate the sophistication of what Marketing does for them. As a marketing executive, the speaker portrayed the telltale feeling of superiority that salespeople so often complain about in the early stages of the collaborative process. This pernicious assumption is based upon a privileging of formally recognized theoretical knowledge over practical experience. Because the woman in question had gone to university, gained a tertiary qualification and was now formally recognized as an expert in her field, she felt that she had earned respect and success. In contrast, the sales reps she was denigrating were, to her way of thinking, little more than street hustlers with a bag of tricks and cons that they could use to convince customers to make a purchase. This hardly paints a flattering picture of her opinion of the organization's products, let alone the organization's clients.

The more I encountered these kinds of pernicious inter-departmental hostilities, the clearer it became that something had to be done to improve the situation – and fast! Since the sales function has been all but excluded from post-secondary curricula, the education hurdle has long been one that collaborators have had to work around innovatively, but there is good news on this front: I am fortunate enough to have found a sympathetic ear in the ivied halls: The head of the Executive MBA program at a respected Australian university has seen the light, and I am proud to say that the institution and I are now working together to include a discrete focus on Sales not only in their MBA but also in their Executive MBA curriculum. We are even talking about a graduate or maybe post-graduate qualification in Sales Management as a stand-alone subject. Given the antipathy with which most marketing lecturers view sales this is revolutionary stuff!

I hope that the strides being made in the education arena will, in time, lead to sales reps and marketers who can boast similar levels of qualification. But there is much more to the problem than education. Early in my assessment of the issue, I recognized that there is a lack of motivation for salespeople and marketers to work together in concert. If I could find a way to make them want to work together, to show them, for instance, how they could increase their own productivity through inter-departmental cooperation, the path to collaboration would be lit up like an airport's runways at night.

I wasn't the only (or even the first) person to recognize the urgency of the problem. The other solutions on the market, though, were point solutions – they addressed specific problems between Sales and Marketing, while ignoring the issue burning at the heart of the disconnect. They boasted about their narrow results, but when I looked at them in more detail I recognized them for what they really were.

Point solutions can remediate some of the symptoms but they cannot cure the illness. They are, at best, topical ointments, at worst, placebos.

I have listed below some of these point solutions. This list is by no means exhaustive, nor is it in any particular order, but it will give you some idea as to the range of choices that I encountered when I first started looking at possible solutions to collaborative problems. Many of these are still being presented to organizations today:

Sales Training

There are hundreds, if not thousands, of sales methods out there to choose from, from the older – some would say tried and tested – SPIN selling and Miller-Heiman methods, to some of the more recently popular ones, which include solution/consultative selling and provocative, challenger, disruptive, and collaborative selling.

Sales Coaching

This is ongoing advice and mentoring offered to and for individual reps that often pertains to specific sales opportunities and is usually conducted as an adjunct to sales training.

Sales and Marketing Messaging

Also sometimes known as 'power messaging', it is designed to align the messages that Sales and Marketing use so as to speak to the market with a consistent voice. In my opinion, this sounds like the start of a solution, but, in practice, it does little more than paper over the deep cracks that exist between Sales and Marketing.

Marketing Strategy Consulting

This is advice that may range from the higher-level strategy such as go-to-market strategy, product strategy, pricing strategy, segmentation/targeting/positioning strategy, outbound/inbound and content marketing strategy. As with so many services, there are good consultants and there are bad ones.

Leadership Coaching

This addresses the difference between managing and leading. In the context of Sales+Marketing Collaboration, successful sales reps are often promoted to become sales managers. So far so good, but they have never really needed to acquire the skillset that helps them to lead people. Leadership coaches teach emerging and new managers (or, occasionally, old ones) how to lead and – importantly - how to apply their newfound skills effectively.

CRM Systems

These are customer relationship management systems that help users to keep track of sales opportunities, leads follow up and individual reps' progress on their sales activities. They also provide sales forecast reports, which predict future sales across individual reps, the entire sales force or more specific criteria, such as geography, product, etc.

Sales Force Automation Systems

These are created to take some of the burden of menial tasks off of the sales force and to provide activity reports and forecasts.

Marketing Automation Systems

These are meant to attract more prospects to the organization while they are on their Buyer's Journey. They do so by responding to prospects automatically with the appropriate content until they are ready to contact a sales rep. They can also be used to capture each visitor's identity and navigation history so that when the visitor makes contact, your reps are forearmed with information about the prospect's potential interest areas.

Sales Support Systems

These support reps in the field or in front of a prospect with on-demand sales information and related content so that they have immediate access to relevant content that is tailored to prospects' requirements.

Website Content Automation Systems

These are designed to make the most of your vast content and to tailor it to suit your website's individual visitors. Depending on the visitor's past viewing history, the system changes what the website displays to that visitor, which can (and often does) entice them to stay longer. Some of these systems can offer visitors targeted suggestions as to what web content may be of interest to them next.

Despite mountains of evidence to the contrary, providers of all these offerings that I have listed above claim to varying degrees that their solutions will produce complete (or nearly complete) 'Sales and Marketing Alignment'. The fact that this has become something of a buzzword in recent years makes it clear that organizations (and those that cater to them) are starting to recognize that misalignment is a serious issue that can no longer be ignored.

What all of these point solutions miss is the human element in the equation. They may apply a balm to the sore area (i.e. the symptom), but they don't address the underlying cause of the disconnect between Sales and Marketing.

It seems to me that alignment is one thing but, surely, there can be no guarantee of success unless the people involved are motivated at a personal level to work together towards a common goal. I'll say it again in a slightly different way: You can have the most sophisticated processes and the latest technology, but if your people are not working together, all your efforts will come to nothing.

We are awash in point solutions, but none of these offer a holistic way that addresses the People, Processes and Technology elements in the right sequence and in the right order of priority. The moment I recognized this, a burning passion was kindled in me to locate the precise balance of these elements that could close the gap between Sales and Marketing. With this passion as my starting point, I developed, tested, and refined the solution you hold in your hands: the OneTEAM Method™.

To the best of my knowledge, I am the first to offer a dedicated method to help the PEOPLE on both sides of the sales and marketing divide to recognize and understand the important roles that their counterparts play, how they are different, how to make best use of their differing skill sets and competencies, and how to teach them how they can come together as one team to benefit themselves and the entire organization.

We need to get away from a silo mindset where Sales and Marketing operate largely independently from each other with no shared processes or metrics. What most vendors advocate ('Sales Enablement' or 'Sales and Marketing Alignment') is really nothing much more than a focus on discrete and narrow processes, mostly on lead generation and management. I want organizations to get away from this narrow process mindset and to strive for a holistic collaboration mindset.

I have tried to illustrate this journey for you here:

At the risk of overstating the point here, we need to go beyond mere Sales and Marketing alignment. We need to go up one level and strive for Sales+Marketing Collaboration.

Collaboration happens between people, it makes work more enjoyable, it gives that spice that makes people want to come to work, to do great things together, to achieve and to succeed as a team. I hanker to create business environments where people are keen to support and help each other to become the best that they can be. I want people to thrive on a garden bed of collaboration in an atmosphere where all the third party point solutions I mentioned above can really help both the people and the processes to flourish.

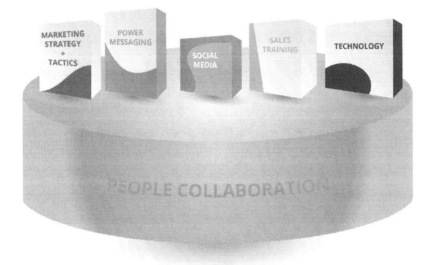

We are, after all, not robots; we are human, and humans are more complicated than mere processes and metrics. We are ambitious, proud and fearful. We crave recognition, fulfillment and satisfaction. Processes and technologies simply cannot account for these on their own. We need to go deeper, to a more fundamental place – to the human heart at the center of the problem.

My OneTEAM Method™ does this.

It, and it alone, builds a solid collaboration foundation, without which point solutions cannot hope to be more than just passingly successful.

It does this by recognizing that without addressing the people aspect first, all the point solutions in the world will simply not deliver the expected results.

In short, it has a heart.

Chapter Takeaway

Throughout this book and in this chapter I make a somewhat impassioned plea in favor of collaboration. It is this same passion that inspires my writing, my speaking, my coaching and my consulting work. It led me to develop the OneTEAM Method™ and to help organizations like yours onto the path to collaborative success and to the great enjoyment that comes with working in a collaborative team environment.

Chapter 15:
What Does The OneTEAM
Method™ Achieve?

As I mentioned previously, the OneTEAM Method™ opens up previously dammed communication channels between two of the most customer-facing departments in any organization, namely Sales and Marketing. It is all about helping these two important teams come back together and act as one again. Before moving on to the Method itself, let's take a closer look at some of the benefits that you can expect if you implement the OneTEAM Method™.

1. Clearer Communication through breaking down Barriers

The OneTEAM Method™ solves problems in any organization in which the communication between Sales and Marketing is less than ideal.

Sales may know how to sell, and Marketing may know how to market, meaning they both know how to speak to people outside of the organization, but they might need a little guidance talking to each other in more productive ways.

The OneTEAM Method™ provides that structure.

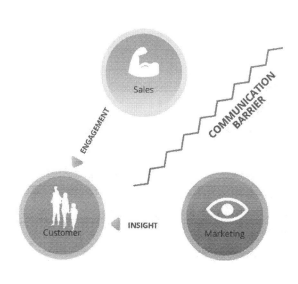

Of course, in situations where it becomes clear that Sales, Marketing, or both can reap substantial benefits from further training or coaching that may be less related to best practice collaboration (such as sales training, leadership coaching, or marketing consulting for instance) my method will make these support tools so much more effective than they would be otherwise.

2. Better Collaboration through 360-Degree Feedback

The OneTEAM Method™ establishes a 360-degree continuous feedback loop between Sales and Marketing so that they can collaborate more easily and much more effectively. But it also goes further as it can now also include feedback from your customers, which is really interesting if you want to know how your marketing messages and your sales efforts are being perceived by your target audience. .

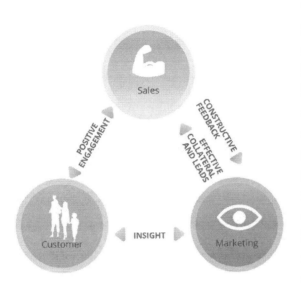

The 360-Degree Collaboration loop ensures that Sales can keep Marketing informed on which marketing support really works for them, and which, in turn, allows Marketing to focus on doing more of what is working for Sales and less of what isn't. Each team can now focus on its own competencies, yet support the other in working towards a more positive business outcome for all parties involved.

You may even choose to also include your customers in this collaboration.

The OneTEAM Method™ becomes really powerful for organizations that are brave enough to include some of their key customers in the feedback loop. While some executives might fear that this arrangement may open up the organization to the airing of their dirty linen, it also brings a powerful sense of partnership to the vendor-client relationship beyond just the internal Sales+Marketing Collaboration question – it's a classical win-win-win scenario, and who wouldn't want that?

3. Maintaining a Fully Collaborative Enterprize

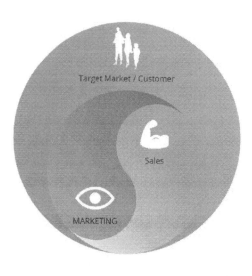

Through the power of the OneTEAM Method™, we end up with an organization where the lines between Sales and Marketing blur to the point that they become almost indistinguishable from the outside.

They are like each other's yin and yang.
They work as OneTEAM.
They are far more effective.
They collaborate with each other and with their key customers.
They achieve results, both in financial and in human terms.
And they enjoy their work like never before.

4. Improved Sales Performance through better Support

As you might guess, a structured program that drives Sales and Marketing effectiveness results in a substantially more effective sales force. I have found that the most compelling case for implementation hinges upon this point, so the rest of the points in this chapter will include calculations showing you exactly what kind of ROI those implementing the OneTeam Method™ can expect.

Key to these figures is the understanding that incremental improvement to a single function can lead to sometimes-dramatic holistic improvements. For long-time readers of business literature, this will not come as a new revelation. Back in 1992, Stephen Hindman and John Sviokla from the Harvard Business School looked into sales effectiveness and found that: *"A company that can increase its sales-revenue-per-person productivity by just 5%, can increase its profit results by 20%."*

In other words, sales productivity is a four-fold profit multiplier!

The impact of this statement can easily be demonstrated in a quick sample calculation.

In the table below please compare the top line and bottom line results when varying the organization's focus on specific objectives.

In the case here, we are comparing the financial impact of reducing direct selling expenses against increasing the sales volume, and against raising the price. At first glance it looks like raising prices is the best option. And it probably is from a purely financial perspective, but in the modern ultra-competitive climate it is not always realistic.

The table is meant to highlight that only a small change in the right parameter can make a big difference for an organization.

P&L Performance Impact	Base Case P&L	Reduce Direct Selling Expenses by 5%	Increase Sales Vloume by 5%	Raise Price by 5%
Sales Revenue	$100.00	$100.00	$105.00	$105.00
Cost of Goods Sold (COGS)	$60.00	$60.00	$63.00	$60.00
Gross Profit	$40.00	$40.00	$42.00	$45.00
Fixed Costs	$13.00	$13.00	$13.00	$13.00
General Admin Costs	$11.00	$11.00	$11.00	$11.00
Direct Selling Expenses	$6.00	$5.70	$6.00	$6.00
Profit Before Tax (PBT) in $	$10.00	$10.30	$12.00	$15.00
Profit Before Tax (PBT) Increase from Base Case in $	$0.00	$0.30	$2.00	$5.00
Profit Before Tax (PBT) Increase from Base Case in %	**0.0%**	**3.0%**	**20.0%**	**50.0%**

Watch out though, because the positive effects that I have outlined above can have an equally amplifying effect when they go into negative territory (i.e. a small discount by a lazy sales rep can have a large negative impact on profitability). Be mindful of that matter.

5. Increased Sales Revenue through Focus

Not all salespeople are alike, so, within any organization, there are top performers and what I like to call second- and third-tier performers. Though such is not always the case, let us for simplicity's sake assume that the top-tier salespeople's performance cannot be substantially improved. There is, however, a great deal of room for improvement in the bottom groups. Here is a sample calculation based on a hypothetical organization:

1. The top performing tier of salespeople brings in $20m in annual sales revenue
2. The remaining salespeople bring in $50m per year

Now let's assume that the OneTEAM Method will even just marginally improve the performance of the middle and bottom groups of salespeople. We're not talking about a 20% or even a 30% leap in productivity here, let's look at just a *very conservative* 5% improvement. What would that accomplish?

Qvidian recently made the following claim: "A five percent gain in the middle 60 per cent of your sales performers," they said, "can deliver over 91 per cent greater sales than a five per cent shift in your top 20 per cent." Across-the-board knowledge sharing – especially when this knowledge is the product of Sales+Marketing Collaboration-enabled dialogue – can substantially impact the bottom 80% of your sales force, enabling and empowering them with the agility and collateral they need to lift their performance considerably.

This means that extracting your top performers' personal sales know-how and corporate knowledge, and transferring it to reps further down the chain is proven to lift the performance of lesser-performing reps and can have untold positive productivity benefits.

Here is the corresponding sample calculation for a fictitious sales organization with $100m in annual revenue. For illustration purposes I have kept the sales targets and rep numbers constant in the before and after scenarios:

	Before OneTEAM Method (Baseline)	After OneTEAM Method Year 1
Annual Sales Target (assume constant)	$100,000,000	$107,000,000
# of Salespeople (assume constant)	100	100
Total Sales Team Revenue Contribution (assume constant)	$30,000,000	$30,000,000
2nd Rate Sales Team Revenue Contribution	$60,000,000	$66,000,000
Bottom Sales Team Revenue Contribution	$10,000,000	$11,000,000
Total Actual Sales	$100,000,000	$107,000,000
Revenue Increase due to sales effectiveness of the bottom and mid-level team increased by just 5%		**$7,000,000**
Sales Profit it at 30% margin		**$21,000,000**

The simple calculation shows that this will result in $7m worth of additional sales revenue per year, and, assuming a gross margin of 30%, the client would be rewarded with $2.1 million more profit!

How would you like additional revenue and more profit each year?

6. Fewer Lost or "No Decision" Sales through Improved Sales Force Confidence

For comparison purposes we are assuming here the same size of organization as in the example above. Additionally, we are assuming that the OneTEAM Method™ can improve the confidence and ability of the sales force to build more effective relationships with its prospects to unstick a *very conservative* 5% of previously lost or 'no decision' sales per year.

If OneTEAM Method™ can reduce the number of lost or stuck sales by just 5% then in our example it will result in a revenue increase of over $3 million and $1 million in additional profit per year! As you can see, even a small improvement in the support that the sales force receives from Marketing will have a dramatic effect on the organization's overall financial health.

Here is the sample calculation:

	Before OneTEAM Method Baseline	After OneTEAM Method 1st Yr
Annual Sales Target	$100,000,000	$107,000,000
How many Salespeople	100	100
Avg Sales Price per Solution	$20,000	$20,000
Avg Sale Closing Rate	33.33%	33.33%
# of Sales Pursuits per year required	$15,000	$15,000
Avg "No Decision" or Lost Sales per year	$10,000	$10,000
Number of 5% fewer poorly qualified Sales Pursuits per year	500	500
Resulting in Additional Closing per year	166.7	166.7
Additional Sales Revenue per year	$ 3,333,350	$ 3,333,350
Sales profit at 30% margin		$ 1,000,005

7. Defrayed Risk through Knowledge Transfer

Let's look at the risk side of the equation.

It is an age-old problem that your star employees go home at the end of each workday with a wealth of corporate know-how and information locked away in their heads. What if they leave and go to your competitor? What would happen if your organization were to *fall behind* competitors that are adopting Sales+Marketing Collaboration initiatives?

A joint research venture between MathMarketing and Marketo showed that alignment between Sales and Marketing departments on sales lead generation and management resulted in a 67% higher probability that marketing-generated leads result in new revenue (http://www.marketo.com/reports/2013-sales-and-marketing-alignment-study/).

If these numbers are true just for this narrow band of sales lead-related interactions, can you imagine what the OneTEAM Method™ could achieve across the board for an organization?

Here is a sample calculation:

If an organization with $100m in annual revenue can lift its sales performance by just 5% then the difference is $5m more revenue and 1.5m more gross profit!

An organization with $100m in annual revenue can lift its sales performance by just 5%. The difference is $5m more revenue and 1.5m more gross profit.

Now look at the red numbers.

If sales performance were to *drop* by just 5% then that would result in $5m lost revenue and 16% less profit!

What would losses like this mean for you and your organization?

If you like, you can estimate the potential financial effect of the OneTEAM Method™ on your own organization's financial results on our website. Just look for the ROI Check there.

Our Total Annual Sales Revenue	$100,000,000			
The Number of our Direct and Indirect Sales Reps	50			
Our Average Gross Profit Margin in percent	30%			
How much can sales revenue increase if our Sales and Marketing teams help each other more?	5%			
What happens if we do nothing?	5%			

Current

Annual Sales Revenue	$100,000,000
Annual Sales Gross Profit	$30,000,000

Potential Result when Deploying the OneTEAM Method	**Total Result**		**Increase**
New Annual Sales Revenue	$105,000,000	New Estimated Sales Revenue Boost Per Year	$5,000,000
New Annual Sales Gross Profit	$31,500,000	New Sales Gross Profit Boost Per Year	$1,500,000
New Annual Sales Revenue	$2,100,000	New Annual Sales Revenue Boost per Rep	$100,000

Potential Loss when ignoring the OneTEAM Method	**Total Result**		**Decrease**
Lower Annual Sales Revenue	$95,000,000	New Estimated Sales Revenue **Loss** Per Year	$-5,000,000
Lower Annual Sales Gross Profit	$28,500,000	New Sales Gross Profit **Loss** Per Year	$-1,500,000
Lower Annual Sales Revenue per Rep	$1,900,000	New Annual Sales Revenue **Loss** per Rep	$-100,000

8. Attracts and Retains Top Talent through a Team Spirit

No matter how in-demand your product or service, without a world-class staff to locate, nurture, and maintain relationships with your customers, you'll consistently fall short of greatness. True business success means the ability to attract, train and retain the best and brightest people around.

Apart from remuneration, the key to attracting and keeping top-rate talent lies in a positive culture. Ontario's OYG Inc. says that, if you want to attract and retain quality talent, the most important thing you can do is "understand your current culture".

This can hardly come as a surprise.

Where would you rather work? In a bellicose culture where people go to battle with each other every day, or in a cooperative and collaborative culture, one in which staff not only help each other, they actually want their co-workers (even those in different departments) to succeed.

The ability to establish a culture-based reputation endows an organization with the power to attract and retain high-performing salespeople, which itself delivers real dollar benefits to an organization. The OneTEAM Method™ includes a series of financial models that helps our clients to identify their low hanging fruit and accordingly to priorities the method implementation.

9. Enhances the Customer Experience through Consistency

I have talked about the Buyer's Journey in which buyers conduct their own research until they feel ready to talk to a sales rep. I also mentioned how critically important it is that the messaging of the online content matches that of the sales rep when the buyer is ready to talk. Nothing much puts a potential buyer off more than confused messaging.

Through Sales+Marketing Collaboration the OneTEAM Method™ ensures that the messaging between online content and personal experience remains consistent and it thus addresses the risk of disconnect at this critical juncture in the Buyer's Journey.

The benefits that collaboration brings in its wake are many, and it can have substantial flow-on effects: a collaborative spirit infuses almost everything that a company does, and customers notice it.

Chapter Takeaway

It is probably not realistic to expect all of the benefits that I have listed to come through at the same time, but it is obvious that these benefits are accumulative and substantial. If you want to know the risk that your organization is taking by *not* adopting Sales+Marketing Collaboration initiatives then simply take the sample calculations above, input your own organization's figures and apply a *negative* percentage.

The results may shock you.

Chapter 16:
OneTEAM Method™ Philosophy

The dictionary defines 'philosophy' thus:

Philosophy

fi 'lo sə fi

Noun

1. the study of the fundamental nature of knowledge, reality and existence, especially when considered as an academic discipline

2. the theory or attitude that acts as a guiding principle for behavior

When I use the term 'philosophy', I do so according to the second definition above. I mean philosophy as a guiding principle. The philosophy that animates the OneTEAM Method™ is the belief that teams working together towards a common outcome is better than individuals working independently and hoping that it will all somehow come together in the end. In other words, teamwork is better than isolation; collaboration is better than silo-ation. The phrase "hope is not a strategy," attributed to former New York City Mayor Rudy Giuliani, really applies in this context. We want – indeed, we need – more than hope.

We want results. What results do we want?

Financial Results

Of course, being in business means that we want financial results, such as revenue growth, profit and we want to deliver value for our shareholders. We measure these results in terms of dollars and cents.

External Recognition

We also want less tangible results in the form of customer satisfaction and loyalty, brand profile and thought leadership. Being less tangible, they are harder to measure, but there are techniques available that can help us to understand how well or poorly we are doing in this respect.

Internal Recognition

In addition to these two, we also want our employees to be happy and engaged in our business. We want them to be good ambassadors for our organization, and high levels of job satisfaction virtually guarantee they will be so. Often, we measure these results in terms of Net Promoter Score or other means.

It seems perfectly logical that we measure these three very differing benefits in their own discrete ways. Equally logical is that we assign achievement targets with key performance indicators (KPIs) to each one. Thus, we have given focus to the teams that are charged with pursuing the results that we are looking for.

The problem is that in many large organizations communication channels between Sales and Marketing departments have been allowed to become dammed up. The distance between Sales and Marketing oftentimes seems harder than ever to bridge, and narrow perspectives and blinkered thinking were able to become entrenched. It is time to pull this siloed approach and the thinking behind it out by the roots.

This is where the philosophy behind the OneTEAM Method™ comes in. The changing habits of buyers have necessitated a change to the way that organizations manage the interactions between Sales and Marketing. These two teams need to work together as one, identifying and striving together to reach a common goal.

A collaboration-first philosophy makes pinpointing the place on the map that we want to reach fairly easy. Once we have our bearings and know where we are going, all we need is the route. Here it is: Open up the bidirectional channels of communication so that Sales and Marketing can collaborate more effectively.

This constructive feedback loop (its ideation, its implementation, its maintenance) is so important to me that it has come to touch nearly every aspect of my professional life. You can even see its power reflected in our corporate logo. The two arcs, representing Sales and Marketing, come together to form a collaborative circle of shining gold.

I love it for its simplicity and the deep and powerful meaning that lies behind it for me.

The OneTEAM Method™ delivers a solution that brings people together in ways they often find surprising. Perhaps most surprising is the fact that it helps those who might have been standing in their own way to *become the solution.*

Yes, the People can become the solution.

Allowing the very people who are most immediately and often negatively affected by the siloed approach to play a part in the development of the solution means that there will be little resistance when it comes to implementing that solution. The buy-in takes place at a much deeper level than it would if the solution were (as it so often is) imposed on them from above.

It sets the teams up for true collaboration and forms the basis for the underlying principle of the OneTEAM Method™. As is so often the case, the simplest solutions are often the most effective. And so it is with the OneTEAM Method™.

The essence of the OneTEAM Method™ is very simple. Here is in its most basic form:

> **Sales supports Marketing, and Marketing supports Sales.**

It's all about showing these two important business teams how they can come together and act as one again.

Chapter Takeaway

The philosophy behind the OneTEAM Method™ is based on the fundamental belief that collaboration is better than isolation. One would think that this is axiomatic.

So why is it then that collaboration is not as ubiquitous as it could be?

Peter Strohkorb

Chapter 17:
A World First: The OneTEAM Method™ Collaboration Index

Most organizations that I have encountered – especially those that bring me on board to facilitate an effective implementation of the OneTEAM Method™ – are at least mid-way through their collaborative journey. Thankfully, few organizations are content to let their sales and marketing teams operate *entirely* independently for too long.

All organizations fall somewhere on what I call the Collaboration Maturity Spectrum. Before we turn to look at the Collaboration Index itself, let's first look at the aforementioned Spectrum that underpins the Index.

If the Spectrum moves from left to right, the stage furthest to the left represents the lowest amount of collaborative maturity.

This stage I call the 'Silo Mindset'. It is characterized by a completely (or nearly completely) siloed approach to Sales+Marketing Collaboration.

Silo Mindset

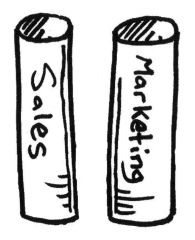

The two departments (un)happily co-exist without much substantive interaction. Marketing throws sales leads and collateral over the fence to Sales, then wipes its hands, absolving itself of any downstream consequences.

Without any kind of usable feedback loop in place, the dialogue (when there is any) is often disrespectful and frustrating for both parties. Any criticism leveled at Marketing by Sales is met with a complete shirking of responsibility: "We've done our work," says Marketing, "now it's up to Sales to sell."

The next maturity stage in the Collaboration Maturity Spectrum is the mid-point, halfway between the un-collaborative environment that I described above and the highly collaborative one I'll describe below. I call this mid-way point the 'Process Mindset'.

At this point, each department has realized that collaboration is better (i.e. more beneficial and profitable) than separation.

At this stage, Sales and Marketing are working together, albeit in a limited way, usually along a small set of narrowly defined business processes.

The most popular of these seems to be the generation, nurturing and management of marketing-generated sales leads.

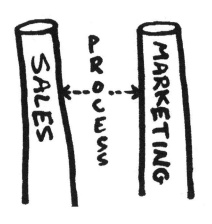

PRocess Mindset

What often stalls organizations in this stage of the Maturity Spectrum is their tendency to treat these initial collaborative stages as something of a one-way street, satisfying one party at the expense of the other. Since the Process Mindset is much harder to break out of than the Silo Mindset, the mid-point in the collaborative journey is the point at which many would-be collaborators stall. What keeps them from maturing completely is the narrow, process-obsessed and blinkered approach. The broader the engagement between Sales and Marketing and the more that information begins to flow in both directions, the easier the transition will be to the most mature stage in the collaborative spectrum.

The really mature organizations understand that there is much more to marketing than the generation of sales leads and marketing content and that there is more to sales than the relatively efficient and effective use of those leads and that content. I am talking here about important aspects of marketing such as brand recognition and profile, organizational thought leadership, market awareness, early trend spotting, ideal target/customer profiling, market segmentation/targeting/positioning, etc. There is so much more to marketing than the mere generation and hand over of sales leads.

What I call the 'Collaboration Mindset' encompasses all these points and more. It is not so much an end point as it is an understanding on the part of all stakeholders that Sales and Marketing need to be in a constant state of dialogue and that this dialogue must be at all times moving towards a mutually-beneficial outcome.

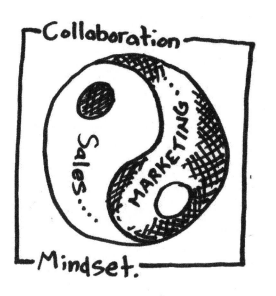

The Collaboration Mindset means that consultation is not demanded, it is sought.

Collaboration is pervasive and no longer something that is mandated from on high. Most importantly, the collaborative practices that are in place significantly impact both the customers' experience and the employees' productivity, and job satisfaction.

The Collaboration Mindset (and the practices it brings with it) is the best possible way for organizations to do what they long ago set out to do, namely to improve productivity through team work.

It is the best way to live the term 'Smarketing'.

By the way, *smarketing* is a real term. Try googling it and you might be surprised at the search results. I have trade marked the term in Australia as to me it so aptly describes the Sales+Collaboration mindset.

But how do you know when you have arrived at this nirvana, or how far your organization has yet to go to reach it?

The old business adage that you can't manage what you can't measure, applies here, too.

At Peter Strohkorb Consulting International we have recently developed something that we believe is a world first.

What we managed to do is to reduce all the complexity that surrounds the measurement of Sales+Marketing Collaboration quality, and express it as a single numeric value: one number that reflects an organization's Sales+Marketing Collaboration maturity.

We call it the OneTEAM Method™ Collaboration Index, or CI for short.

The CI condenses the various factors that go into collaborative success into a single, easy-to-understand figure that tells you in no uncertain terms how well – or how poorly – your teams are collaborating.

For the first time, would-be collaborators have a tool at their disposal that allows them, not only to benchmark their organization against best practice, peers and competitors, but also to show where improvement is still needed.

Here is what a typical OneTEAM Method™ Collaboration Index result looks like:

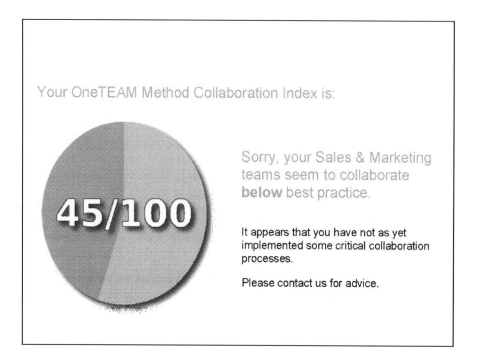

Chapter Takeaway

Being able to measure, compare and benchmark the quality of Sales+Marketing Collaboration in an organization is extremely important if you want to repair the relationship between Sales and Marketing. As the saying goes, you can't manage what you can't measure. Now you can measure collaboration quality and, with that measurement in hand, you can know – perhaps for the first time – precisely how you should be proceeding.

Let us know if you are curious about the Collaboration Index of your organization.

Chapter 18:
OneTEAM Method™ Productivity Trinity

With over 15 years of B2B Sales and Marketing executive experience at some of the largest corporations on the planet, such as SONY, 3M, Canon and CSC, I have witnessed dozens of different approaches, each of them attempting to effect change as quickly and efficiently as possible. Approaches ran the gamut from scientific to hopeful, productive to evasive, successful to – shall we say – less than successful.

About six years ago, I began to recognize a pattern in the most successful of these collaboration models. When I began to advise organizations on, and guide them to, collaborative success, it became clear that the underlying patterns that I recognized were not coincidental. Out of this long period of observation came the OneTEAM Productivity Trinity and eventually the OneTEAM Method™. The first of these recognizes that effective Sales/Marketing partnerships are built upon a three-tier plinth of People, Processes, and Technology. The second is a proven method for addressing and engaging each of these business elements to produce a dynamic, synergistic environment that is conducive in every way to both short-term and long-term success.

Take sales lead generation as an example.

Let's say an organization has decided that Marketing will generate the sales leads for Sales to follow up. Using today's jargon, these leads are usually referred to as "Marketing-Qualified-Leads" (MQLs). If sales lead quantity is the only criterion by which Marketing is judged, you'll often find self-congratulating marketing departments, who feel their job is done when they make their MQL numbers, who care too much about the entrance to the sales pipeline or funnel and not enough about how well their leads convert into actual sales. The same narrow definitions of success can see sales departments celebrating when they meet sales quotas when the business' market share or profitability is stagnant or even dropping. It is precisely this kind of poor collaboration that, according to <u>Philip Kotler in the Harvard Business Review,</u> "raises market-entry costs, lengthens sales cycles, and increases the cost of sales." (<u>http://hbr.org/2006/07/ending-the-war-between-sales-and-marketing/ar/1</u>).

A collaborative Sales+Marketing relationship entails a movement from 'your' problem or 'their' problem to 'our' problem, i.e. one that seeks a collective solution to collective issues. By no means does this necessarily mean that sales and marketing departments should be merged into a single department. Solutions that attempt to erase the distinction between the two functions (and, just as crucially, the personalities that dominate therein) often only exacerbate the problem.

Effective Sales+Marketing Collaboration is not about doing away with specialized departmental functions, but it *is* necessary to eliminate the all-too-common barriers that stand in the way of effective inter-departmental communication. The goal is to build high-functioning inter-departmental partnerships, and a lack of specialization doesn't produce the kinds of results we are aspiring to.

I find it helpful to think of what separates Sales from Marketing as something softer, perhaps a finely woven but transparent curtain, one that facilitates the movement of ideas between both departments, one through which each department can see what the other is doing, one through which positive and negative feedback can pass without a great deal of friction, and one where the functions are clearly defined even though they may partially overlap. This kind of relationship often involves integration through all stages of the sales funnel, meaning that Sales and Marketing each have their parts to play throughout the various stages of the customer/organization interaction. They work through these stages together, as one team.

If we want to accomplish this, we first need to understand that *some* degree of tension between Sales and Marketing is healthy. The strategies that we will cover in the next chapter are not about entirely eliminating this friction; they attempt to manage it to a point where it becomes constructive, highly effective, and eliminates 'group think', i.e. the tendency of a group of like-minded people to see things all in the same way. Group think means that bad ideas go unchallenged, whereas input from a broad range of perspectives and constructive friction (pushback for example) is necessary for healthy decision-making.

Just as high-quality motor oil enhances performance in a motor vehicle, a good collaborative strategy can do the same for an organization. Neither eliminates friction altogether, but they dramatically reduce its negative effects. Collaborative strategies and high-quality motor oil are both compounds that if applied in the right areas, will make the engine perform better while, at the same time, keep the moving parts from grinding on each other.

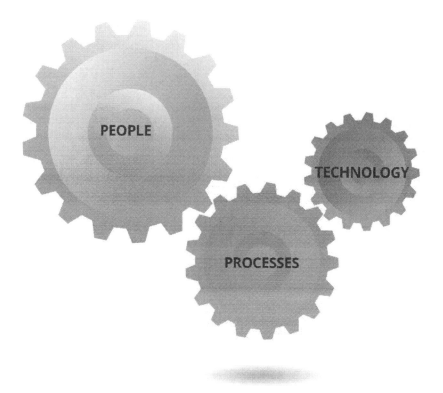

Of course, as I mentioned previously, we are dealing with people, not machines. This simple and glaringly obvious point seems to be lost on many of today's would-be collaborators. Why, for instance, do I continue to see projects where the implementation of technology receives far more attention than the people that will be using it?

Too many (far, far too many) large organizations are trying to solve a people problem with a technological solution.

If people aren't talking to each other, then it is most likely not because they lack the means to do so. No, it is almost always because, for whatever reason, they are not inclined or even willing to talk to each other. To resolve the issue at the heart of harmful collaborative friction you need to start with the *people* dimension first.

This is what the OneTeam Method™ Productivity Trinity is all about.

It makes sure that the grease goes in the right places. It focuses first and foremost on the People in an organization. Thereafter, it looks at the Processes and finally the Technology that they use:

People, Processes, and Technology, that is the right order of priority.

Extensive experience and research has proven time and again that this is the way that organizations can build a lasting foundation upon which further collaborative strategies can be built. Implementing my method without the guiding hand of the Productivity Trinity puts the cart before the horse. Let's now take a closer look at each of the three components of the Productivity Trinity.

1. People Power

Let us not forget, when we are implementing any kind of collaborative strategy, we are dealing with human beings, which means we must also deal with all their thoroughly human imperfections and sensitivities.

The human element is not only the most crucial component of the Productivity Trinity; it is also the one most resistant to change. It is for this reason that many would-be collaborators balk at the most crucial moment in the process – namely, addressing the counterproductive habits and mindsets of the individuals within the organization. Let's face the facts: effective Sales+Marketing Collaboration demands change that will touch upon nearly every facet of an organization. Those organizations that have most benefitted from the OneTEAM Method™ are those most willing to place everything – strategies, attitudes, perceptions, processes, and, yes, even corporate culture – under the microscope and possibly under the knife.

Since the term 'culture change' carries with it a host of negative connotations (especially for executives), I have found it best – and most successful – when talking about changing the way that functions interact within an organization to refer to the process as 'cultural alignment'.

No matter what you call it, as long as they go to the root of the problem, small, manageable changes can have powerful effects from top to bottom within an organization. Each of the three steps in the OneTEAM Method™ addresses collaborative issues in this way. This is the reason that the organizations using the Method have enjoyed so much success. Rather than tackling the superficial symptoms of misalignment, we address the deeper causes, clearing the path for a more cooperative and prosperous future unencumbered with the collaborative issues of the past.

Nobody likes to be criticized, but trying to circumvent the human element will never produce the kind of collaborative workplace in which everybody can thrive. The key throughout the OneTEAM Method™ is not to assign blame, belittle each department in turn, or even to highlight problematic behaviors; rather, it is about creating an environment in which collaboration is not only possible, but in which it occurs naturally. This is not to say that less-than-desirable attitudes and behaviors are given a pass. You can't make an omelet without breaking a few eggs; similarly, some bruised egos are almost inevitable, but criticism takes a back seat to constructive problem solving. We want to play the ball, not the man (to use a football analogy). Rather, the focus is on giving the leadership team the tools that they need to improve the inter-functional relationships that are the foundation upon which the collaborative framework stands.

2. Processes and Metrics

Once there is multi-level buy-in in terms of assessing and addressing the crucial human element in the Sales/Marketing alignment issue, the next tier in the Productivity Trinity looks at the processes and metrics, particularly where those processes and metrics are applied to the points at which the two functions most often intersect. These are most likely to be around marketing-generated sales leads and sales collateral.

In the most successful organizations, the processes that traverse this shared Sales/Marketing territory are typically those that leadership tends to visit and revisit regularly. To be effective, any collaborative strategy must fearlessly navigate this territory, enhancing processes and developing joint metrics to continually improve the pipeline quality and quantity, and ultimately the sales outcome.

I have already cited IDC's shocking statistic earlier, but it is worth repeating: *"Only 25% of sales leads and collateral that Marketing creates is ever used by Sales teams."*

My own research and experience in the field confirm this statistic. I have found that it is at this Sales/Marketing intersection that enhanced metrics and aligned objectives can be most impactful. A surprising number of organizations, when they look closely at the existing relationship between Sales and Marketing, recognize that the two departments, in large part thanks to these siloed metrics and objectives, are actually working at cross-purposes or with a large degree of duplication of effort. For goal-alignment to be in place, Marketing's measure of success needs to be tied more closely to sales progress and results, not lead generation alone.

Organizations that rely on a wide-mouthed sales lead pipeline – one in which Marketing is under substantial pressure to produce high numbers of leads – may be harming their bottom line by pressuring Marketing in this way to go for quantity over quality. It is important for Marketing to understand that each one of the leads that are fed into the funnel actually translates into follow-up time spent on the part of Sales, even if it's only a quick touch to determine a lead's viability. This can create a situation where Marketing is meeting its targets, but Sales is struggling to meet theirs due to a significant amount of time spent chasing down unpromising material.

We want Sales and Marketing to pull on the same rope (preferably from the same end), so there needs to be a set of agreed values, definitions, and, finally, metrics that both sides can live with. We want Sales to focus on selling and Marketing to concentrate on marketing. Anything other than this kind of cooperation represents a substantial financial risk in today's competitive markets.

Sales reps preparing their own collateral or modifying existing marketing collateral is a substantial waste of a salesperson's time and energy. By the same token, it is equally unproductive to have Marketing prepare collateral that will never make it into the prospects' or customer's hands. Therefore, improving the relationship between Sales and Marketing can have demonstrable productivity-raising and revenue-boosting effects:

1) Salespeople will spend more of their time selling (not creating marketing collateral)

2) Marketing will create more of the kind of content that Sales will actually use

3) With the right type of collateral (collaboratively created in response to feedback) Sales will accelerate its sales velocity and increase deal closure rates

4) Marketing will enjoy a more productive relationship with Sales, and vice versa

5) Morale will improve, which in turn attracts and retains higher performing talent

Once we have addressed the human element and have achieved consensus then the ensuing processes and metrics follow much more easily than they otherwise would, and the benefits of having everybody on the same page become indisputable.

3. Technology

As I have not been shy about mentioning throughout this book, I approach technology with a degree of caution and I advise others to do the same.

This does not mean that technology doesn't have a role to play in the Trinity and in the Method, but it is the third *and final* tier in the trinity. It is not last because it is un-important. No, it is last because it helps to reinforce and maintain the structure that the other two steps in the Trinity have erected. It comes last, but it is by no means least.

Technology can make information more accessible, it can facilitate dialogue and streamline well-thought-out business processes, but it should always be regarded as a facilitator, not as an end in its own right.

Any approach that seeks technological solutions before addressing the two other elements in the Productivity Trinity is asking for the equivalent of a Sisyphean task.

As the graphic here illustrates, fewer than 15% of organizations achieved improved win rates from implementing sales tools, mobile or otherwise. According to CSO Insights, An astounding 85% of organizations surveyed failed to increase revenue from technology deployments alone, and more than 90% were unable to reduce the time it takes to close a sale (http://www.csoinsights.com/Publications/Shop/Sales-Performance-Optimization).

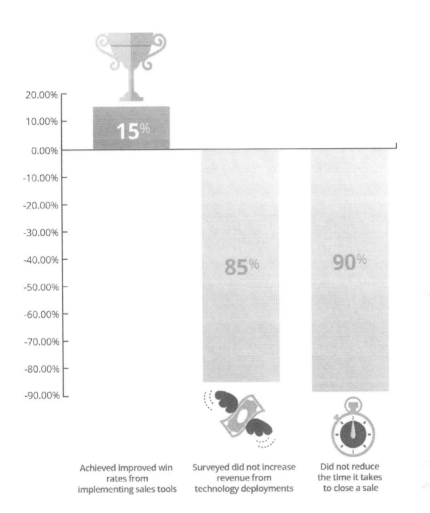

Achieved improved win rates from implementing sales tools	Surveyed did not increase revenue from technology deployments	Did not reduce the time it takes to close a sale

This does not mean that technology itself is the problem.

A wealth of research including some of my own has shown that there is substantial ROI for those who automate well-aligned processes and communication pathways. More often than not, the problem for tech-centric collaborators is the *way* that the solution is rolled out. End users often attempt to use the new technology in the same way that they did the old (often replicating and automating poorly performing processes). If it is the process that is at the root of the problem, automation will only deliver flaws more quickly, not eradicate them for you. The same goes for data: no matter how sophisticated your new technology, feed it with incomplete, incorrect, or inconsistent (so-called 'dirty') data, and the results will inevitably disappoint. After all: bad data in = bad data out.

Finally, under the banners of 'multi-channel strategy' and 'content curation' too many marketing departments automate intending to broadcast as far and wide as possible. Automation tools may well allow for this amplification and broadcasting of, say, an organization's online presence, but the organizations that are finding new technology the most effective are those using the latest tools to target in sophisticated ways smaller, more focused groups of qualified and motivated prospects.

World-leading organizations consistently use technology like a scalpel, not like a flamethrower.

Chapter Takeaway

The OneTEAM Method™ Productivity Trinity recognizes the importance of an approach that puts People first, Processes second, and Technology third. Indeed, this approach is the only way to guarantee that would-be collaborators will see their efforts crowned with success.

Chapter 19:
The OneTEAM Method™ Steps

No two organizations are exactly the same, and they often are at very different stages of maturity along the collaboration spectrum. Some are just starting out on their collaboration journey, while others may already be well on their way.

It is for this reason that I have developed a multi-purpose tool kit that has helped my clients first to understand where their organization sits along the collaboration spectrum and then to provide them with the knowledge and skills that they need to improve their situation and to accelerate their organization's collaboration journey.

In this chapter I will outline the various tools and process steps that my clients have successfully adapted to suit their expectations and requirements. This is not to say that all of the minutiae of these strategies apply equally in all cases; rather, they represent the range of options and problem-specific solutions that my team and I have found to lead to the kind of outcomes that our clients call us in for.

As I have stressed throughout this book, the OneTEAM Method™ takes a radically different approach to the way that large organizations traditionally operate, but its wide-reaching efficacy means that

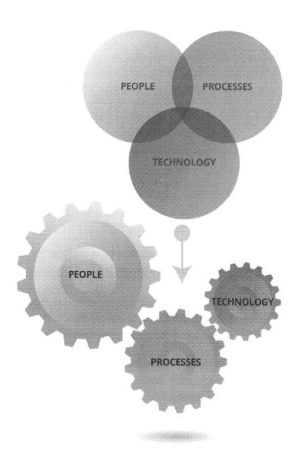

additional point solutions such as sales training that are applied after the OneTEAM Method is implemented will work much more effectively than they otherwise could.

When you get to a point where your Sales and Marketing teams actually *want* to work together they will communicate more effectively and collaborate at a much deeper level than you could ever achieve through CRM or automation systems alone.

Everything else tends to work better too.

Just think about how much more effective your sales training, marketing consulting, leadership coaching and power messaging could be if Sales and Marketing collaborated harmoniously and if they supported each other better.

Above is an illustration that shows just how different my approach to the implementation of collaboration methodology really is.

At the top of the diagram, you see the typical Venn diagram that technology implementers use when describing their focus areas. The three equally sized circles don't really match up to the way that the majority of collaborative solutions on the market are implemented. The reality is, a faithful depiction of technology implementations today would feature a 'Technology' circle that by quite some margin would dwarf the other two.

Perhaps not surprisingly, I have a different perspective on this.

The OneTEAM Method™ first helps the people to *want* to work together, countering entrenched attitudes and preconceptions that may have built up over years of siloed thinking.

We do this by taking our clients through my unique 5-step method. These 5 steps are as follows:

1) Assess

2) Empower

3) Compel

4) Build

5) Maintain

Just as is the case with the Productivity Trinity that I covered in the last chapter, the order of these steps is extremely important.

Let's begin with the first step: Assess.

1. Assess

I have said it before, and I'll say it again: Look before you leap. The first step in the Method is to assess the state of Sales+Marketing Collaboration within your organization. To guide you through the self-assessment process, there are two tools available through my website: the 2-Minute ROI Estimator and the 3-minute Sales+Marketing Collaboration Self-Assessment Test.

a) ROI Self-Assessment

Our ROI Estimator is available free of charge on our website. This tool allows you to input your own sales-related figures and estimate the financial benefit that may result from a given improvement in sales force productivity gained through your implementation of the OneTEAM Method™. If you know your organization well then it only takes about two minutes to complete. All you need to do is to enter the current annual revenue, the number of sales reps in your organization, your average sales margin percentage and your own 'guestimate' of an improvement in sales force productivity that tighter collaboration between Sales and Marketing might deliver to your business.

The Estimator will then return a dollar value, a reflection of the additional revenue and new profit opportunities that the OneTEAM Method™ can help you to achieve. It also calculates the additional revenue per rep so that they can see the additional commission that they can earn when they wholeheartedly commit to the method.

The ROI Estimator is essentially designed as a decision-making tool to help our prospective clients decide for themselves whether or not they should invest time into exploring the deeper business benefits that the OneTEAM Method™ offers. Now, it is available to you free of charge so that you can make that crucial Yes/No decision.

b) Collaboration Self-Assessment

Also available on our website, the Self-Assessment Test is a questionnaire that will help you benchmark, at a high level, your organization's current Sales+Marketing Collaboration level against world's best practice. The test will return a benchmark score that indicates where on the collaboration spectrum your sales and marketing teams currently sit. I recommend that you use it in conjunction with the ROI Estimator tool to gain a more complete picture of your organization's collaborative potential.

Here's a tip: Have your salespeople and your marketing people complete this test separately and then compare the results. Few things illustrate the existence and the size of the gap between Sales and Marketing more than this simple side-by-side comparison.

If you receive a very low score, you may want to look at adopting the OneTEAM Method™ as the proven framework that will help you to change your organization's approach to Sales+Marketing Collaboration in more substantial ways. If, however, you receive an extremely high score, chances are you are already well ahead of the average. You may only need the OneTEAM Method™ to fine-tune your collaborative procedures (and it will do that in spades). Again, this is a high-level 'wet finger in the air' test that can be conducted at any time on our website.

It is simply meant to help you to determine whether or not you wish to explore the OneTEAM Method™ further for your organization. You can find both of the above tests on my website at www.peterstrohkorbconsulting.com. for a nominal fee.

If you want to take the review process yet further, then the next step is:

c) 360-Degree Opportunity Assessment

Many of my clients understand the importance of getting the assessment stage of the method right. As the first step, it is absolutely essential that would-be collaborators gain a rich understanding of their collaborative potential and, perhaps more importantly, of the precise areas that can benefit from closer collaboration.

If you want to include this kind of detail in your considerations, then the 360-degree Opportunity Assessment should be something to seriously consider for your organization.

Naturally, the Opportunity Assessment meticulously scrutinizes both the sales and marketing functions within your organization, but since both Sales and Marketing are customer-facing, it is only logical that the method also takes your customers and prospects into consideration. Combining the perspective of your stakeholders from within and the perspective from outside of your organization gives you a much more complete picture and it allows you to move forward with your collaborative strategies with a high degree of certainty and confidence.

After years of conducting these reviews for my clients, I have noticed something of a pleasantly surprising by-product. Involving your clients and prospects in the evaluation process tends to compel extremely honest feedback. Long-time customers vent a few home truths, speaking more frankly than they might if left to their own devices. Moreover, a lot of these customers appreciate being consulted in this way. They feel valued in being asked their opinions in a much more personal forum than the usual online survey or focus group setting. And they are more open and honest with us (being a neutral party with whom they won't have to preserve an ongoing relationship) than they will with your reps. Oftentimes, the information that we unearth in these anonymized interviews are unbelievably valuable to our clients.

Here's a list of some of the questions the 360-Degree Opportunity Assessment attempts to answer:

- How well are your sales and marketing teams collaborating today? How does this level of collaboration compare to best practice?

- What marketing collateral is Sales actually using?

- What marketing collateral is proving effective? (we look at this from the perspective of Sales and also that of your customers)

- Do your customers feel like your sales and marketing teams are on the same page? Are they, for instance, speaking the same language?

- Where are the opportunities to improve Sales+Marketing Collaboration in your organization?

- What (if any) are the collaborative practices your organization is using to good effect? What collaborative practices are missing or just not working?

- How can processes be better aligned?

- How can Marketing better understand and focus on what really works for Sales?

- What kind of ROI can you expect if you implement the OneTEAM Method™?

The 360-degree Opportunity Assessment is a chargeable service due to the large amount of effort and time that it requires, but the unmatched ability that it gives organizations to take a big-picture snapshot of their collaborative practices and improvement potential makes the investment extremely worthwhile.

Once you have a clear picture of the collaborative landscape (perceived, actual, and potential) in your organization, it is time to move onto the second step in the Method.

2. Empower Sales To Critique Marketing's Output

There's an important distinction to be made here. We want to enable Sales to *critique* – but not to criticize – Marketing. Also, this critique is applied to Marketing's *output*, not to Marketing itself.

This distinction must be upheld if we are to get away from the counterproductive environment of finger-pointing and mutual recrimination. For the OneTEAM Method™ to work, it has to begin with a clear understanding of the difference between constructive feedback and unconstructive criticism.

Sales' feedback to Marketing is encouraged much too little in many organizations, perhaps because it often leans more towards the general than the specific or it is directed at a person, rather than a solvable issue, or simply because the CRM system does not cater to it beyond the reporting on sales leads follow up.

To this point, what little feedback there is from Sales often comes from the more vocal and perhaps frustrated or disillusioned 'hero' reps.

Opinions of this kind are often delivered in a confrontational and sometimes highly personal manner. This is often the result of the traditionally one-directional nature of established feedback channels. Frustration mounts and eventually, maybe even inevitably, manifests itself in unpleasant outbursts.

Feedback channels need to be frequently cleared and they need to promote traffic in *both directions*.

Since feedback channels in poorly aligned organizations often tend to over-represent the voice of a vocal minority of 'hero' sales reps, there needs to be a mechanism in place to encourage *constructive* feedback from *all* reps, regardless of their seniority or their geographic location.

Besides, I have repeatedly found that some of the best ideas come from those who speak the softest. People in remote branches far away from head office and those that are more quiet and reserved by nature often need more than just a seat at the table; they need to be encouraged to offer their opinions and ideas.

Regardless of their location (i.e. whether they are based at head office or in the farthest regions of the organization, whether they are inside sales, outside sales, direct sales or indirect sales) give each and every sales rep a formal channel that allows them to constructively critique the content and support that they are receiving from Marketing. Again, it is important that this empowerment doesn't translate to fruitless broad-brush criticism.

Ask sales reps to start rating Marketing's output on a simple scale of 1 to 5. Optionally, they can also make suggestions as to how marketing content can be improved to better suit the specific ways in which it is being used. They can use this opportunity to ask for additional support, to speak openly and frankly about what has worked, has not worked, is working, or is not working. They can also relay back to Marketing how they are using or would like to use the content and how it can be improved to become more useful or impactful in that context.

Make sure to make these suggestions and ratings highly visible. In order to be effective this process must be as transparent as possible from the outset. This transparency should be universal, making little distinctions of rank or location.

No longer is direct feedback restricted to the vocal minority of head office-based sales reps or to the ones that are located physically near Marketing. Instead, every rep, regardless of rank and location, now has an equal opportunity to speak to Marketing and, perhaps more importantly, to be heard.

The kind of difference this kind of feedback mechanism can effect in a very short time is often nothing short of remarkable. Sales reps who feel appreciated, who feel their opinions are of value, often become key players in the collaborative process.

Sales benefit from the ability to provide qualitative feedback on the entire array of support that it is receiving from Marketing (i.e. more than just the sales leads), as well as being able to suggest improvements and even new initiatives. Marketing benefits from the mining of previously untapped potential. Feedback from Sales soon becomes a valuable resource, one that helps Marketing to hone content to a fine point.

This is not to mean that Marketing will now slavishly follow whatever Sales suggests. Instead, Marketing benefits from the feedback that it is now receiving from the entire sales force on an ongoing basis and finally has the information that it needs to make better-informed decisions on how they can support the sales force more effectively. Crucially, as we'll see in the next step, Marketing too has an important role and a strong voice in the method.

3. Compel Marketing To Respond To Sales' Feedback

I have to start my discussion here with an important distinction. Marketing is *compelled* to react to feedback; they are not *beholden* to Sales.

In many organizations, Marketing is the sender and Sales the receiver: Marketing throws sales material in the form of brochures, white papers, blogs, and leads 'over the fence', and Sales is expected to make the most (ideally without complaint) of this material. I have frequently stressed the importance of a two-way dialogue between Sales and Marketing that gives each department equal footing, so it is important to highlight the fact that Marketing is in no way shut out of, or a victim of the feedback loop. It is only natural for Marketing to defend the quality of its collateral and its sales leads. The feedback that Marketing receives is never intended to be the final word. It merely provides the transparency in terms of the sales force's sentiments that Marketing has hitherto lacked. A constructive feedback channel that is open in both directions allows both departments to make *informed decisions.*

However, the feedback from Sales would soon stop if Marketing did not respond in some palpable way to the new feedback. So, in order to be a truly collaborative system of feedback, Marketing must be *compelled* to respond to Sales' feedback. If sales reps' feedback disappeared into a black hole without response from Marketing, the feedback would not only soon stop again, but the teams would likely go back to their previous modus operandi of mutual distrust and animosity – and we know where that leads.

I have found nothing dams up Sales+Marketing collaborative channels faster than Sales offering unprecedented levels of feedback to Marketing without perceiving any tangible change in the type or quality of marketing collateral or sales leads. For the relationship to be even remotely successful, sales reps need to feel that their feedback is a crucial part of the cross-functional dialogue. They need to feel that they are being listened to. They need to see a tangible difference in the collateral and leads that Marketing is generating. This does not mean that Sales' feedback is gospel; after all, we are after tighter integration, not a master/slave relationship. It does, however, mean that Sales' feedback is a valuable source of market insight and that it should be regarded and treated as such.

The way that the OneTEAM Method™ achieves this is through mutual consent and bargaining between sales and marketing teams. When outlining the strategy within your own organization, it is helpful to create something of a tit-for-tat dialogue. The solution needs to feel like a win-win, and, for the sake of a win, both sides of the debate are usually willing to compromise somewhat. As soon as you have reached a stage where agreement can be reached along the lines of M will do X if S will do Y, then you are well on your way to finding mutually agreeable common ground.

My experience has reinforced my long-held belief that as long as the feedback that Marketing is receiving from Sales is constructive, Marketing's response tends to be constructive as well. The same can be said for unemotional feedback. No matter who is on the giving or the receiving end of feedback, emotional delivery tends to produce an equally emotional response. Given the chance to evaluate specific, constructive, and unemotional feedback from Sales rationally, Marketing can be compelled via joint metrics and common objectives to respond in kind. The kind of feedback channel I am describing here allows Sales to feel and see that they are being heard and that their opinions are valued. On the flip side it enables Marketing access to the precise kinds of information that can make their collateral and leads not only reflect the wants and needs of Sales but as a consequence also make them more successful.

Creating proximity is a great way to break down barriers. Remember the Allen Curve in Chapter 5? Bringing Sales and Marketing together regularly and, if possible, face-to-face can make a huge difference. The trick is to find the organizationally specific balance between meeting too often and meeting too little. In my own research, I found that a particularly statistically significant difference between successful and less successful organizations was the high percentage of financially less successful organizations that admitted to '*never*' having meetings that bring both Sales and Marketing to the table. The more successful organizations have learned that frequent, structured and mediated meetings are a good way to engage both departments in productive dialogue, especially in the early stages of the OneTEAM Method implementation.

For the feedback channels to be effective, meetings must not be grievance free-for-alls. Take the temperature early in these meetings and seek ways to keep things conversational and, as I highlighted above, constructive and unemotional (e.g. "it would work better for us if…" rather than "this is useless because…"). Passionate arguments are rarely as compelling as rational ones, so those who let their passion get the best of them should be shown as early as possible that outbursts and tantrums will not be rewarded.

It often helps to have a neutral mediator who can make sure that finger pointing and chest thumping are kept to a respectable minimum. In a truly collaborative workplace, Marketing and Sales should be self-initiating constructive meetings. The mediator's role should shrink over time to next to nothing. The sooner their effective moderation makes their own presence redundant, the better.

While having meetings is clearly important, the quality of the meetings is even more so. Constructive and collaborative meetings are a direct result of the openly cooperative mindset and practices of those who attend them.

This, to me, is the real differentiator.

If these meetings are to be at all successful (i.e. if they are going to result in a more collaborative workplace), it is important that Sales *experiences* that Marketing is really listening to them (i.e. not just smiling and nodding).

This is the purpose of compelling Marketing to respond to the feedback in the first place.

The best way for Marketing to show Sales that they are hearing them is to respond to Sales' feedback with tangibly better and more responsive support. This may not happen overnight, but by trying to be better, Marketing will eventually hit upon something that Sales will use to good effect. Trial and error should not be avoided. On the contrary, the newly collaborative environment should be one in which making mistakes is not only tolerated but accepted, maybe even welcomed.

Building more effective communication channels begins with the effort, not the results. As numerous studies have shown, the best way to learn is from making mistakes. As long as each mistake is only made once, is learned from, and is not repeated. I am not talking about multi-million dollar mistakes here. I am talking about learned experiences, what some change management consultants have dubbed 'Action Learning' – sophisticated trial and error experiments, really. At a high level we want to take Sales and Marketing on a collaboration trajectory that takes us from conversation to trust, to joint decisions, to shared responsibility, to personal accountability and finally to collaborative ownership of the business outcome

Once feedback channels are established and nurtured, it is time to introduce joint metrics, definitions and overlapping responsibilities. While the entrance to the pipeline is the most important intersection (and the first one you'll want to build shared definitions and metrics around) goal alignment, and to some degree compensation as well, will eventually need to take both ends of the sales pipeline into account. If Marketing is only compensated according to the top end of the sales pipeline or funnel then this fuels complacency and exacerbates the quantity over quality issue that would-be collaborators should always try to avoid.

Any time that processes or metrics are under the microscope, it is crucial to make sure that there is agreement between the parties as to what, precisely, is being measured. There is significant evidence supporting the importance of the words that different departments use to communicate with each other. For instance, Marketo and MathMarketing found that renaming CRM vendor stages after sales process stages resulted in a 46% improvement in Marketing-Qualified Leads (MQL) closure; by adopting the language of the Buyer's Journey,

MQL rose by a further 28% (http://www.marketo.com/reports/2013-sales-and-marketing-alignment-study/).

Once Sales and Marketing are reading and speaking the same language, and once they are on the same page, improvements are almost immediate because of Marketing's renewed buyer-centric vision. The goal is to eventually have an integrated process that centers on the buyer's journey all the way from the initial buyer contact to the closing handshake. You can reasonably expect that customer experience will also improve commensurately with the improved Sales+Marketing Collaboration.

The hardest part may well turn out to be determining to what degree Marketing is accountable for selling. In most organizations, Marketing is measured according to the quantity of sales leads that it generates and then passes on to Sales. This leads to a number of problems:

1) Quantity trumps quality, and blame can be shifted from Marketing to the 'incompetent' salespeople, who are unable to close out the leads that Marketing has supplied.

2) Understandably frustrated with this process, Sales rejects a staggering percentage of Marketing leads as inadequate. If Marketing performance is assessed according to Sales Accepted Leads, this can quickly sour the relationship and dam up communication pathways.

3) Salespeople who are struggling to meet their targets will often gravitate towards only the highest quality and most short-term leads. It is only natural, prevailing wisdom says, to go for the bird in the hand, leaving the birds in the bush to other, less-experienced sales reps who may struggle mightily to reach their

targets. This kind of system can lead to huge numbers of expensively procured sales leads going to waste.

The next step, then, is to compel Marketing to respond in a transparent and open way to the feedback it receives from Sales. It is important not only that Sales can see that that Marketing is listening to them but also that it can directly witness how Marketing is responding to the feedback with tangibly better and more responsive support. By the way, this new collaborative environment should also be one where making mistakes is not only tolerated but accepted, maybe even welcomed.

As long as each mistake is only made once and is not repeated. Also, I am not talking about multi-million dollar mistakes; I am talking about tactical learned experiences. Some management consultants refer to this as 'Action Learning' where we are taking people or teams from initial conversation to agreement, then trust, then decision making, then group responsibility, to individual accountability and finally to outcomes ownership. But it does not need to be as complicated as it may sound in consultant- speak.

For example, it is entirely acceptable to try a few different versions of a brochure with different customers or in different markets to see which one has the highest impact. Equally, there may well be a disagreement even between salespeople regarding the efficacy of a particular campaign or promotion. In those cases it should not be a big problem to run multiple variants on the same theme in different market segments to determine which one works best. So, I suppose if we substituted the word 'mistakes' with 'experiments' then everybody should know what is meant.

Rather than broadly negative feedback (e.g. "Marketing's sales leads and content are useless"), each and every interaction between Sales and Marketing should be an exercise in enhancing the organizational performance and the customer experience, which will not only keep customers in the fold longer but will also attract new ones. The goal is to have a detailed portrait of your ideal customer, ideally a high-volume repeat customer who is so impressed with your organization that they become an advocate and even refer like-minded prospects to you. If necessary, Marketing and Sales may need to re-adjust their messaging in order to more effectively draw in those customers who are in the organization's sweet spot.

Goal alignment, and to some degree compensation as well, have to take both ends of the sales pipeline into account. If Marketing is only compensated according to the top end of the sales pipeline or funnel then this fuels complacency and it exacerbates the quantity-over-quality issue that I mentioned above.

Although a reward structure that is revised towards sales outcomes is rarely something that Marketing departments will greet with great enthusiasm, having take-home pay adjusted so that there are rewards for Marketing's offering of higher *quality* leads and better content for Sales can be in everybody's best interest.

This kind of alignment needs to begin with a collective understanding of terminology. True alignment of processes definition means that not only is 'revenue' a term with agreed-upon parameters, so too is lead generation, nurturing and management, which can be established with the aid of lead-scoring. There are quite a number of lead scoring methods readily available, and most CRM vendors offer these techniques off the shelf.

To me, it matters less which of these my clients choose to deploy than it does having a high level of agreement between Sales and Marketing. The fact *that* they are collaborating is more important to me than which tool they use.

While all the above may sound a little as though the OneTEAM Method™ *imposes* new structures and even pay grades onto sales and marketing teams, nothing could be further from the truth. The entire philosophy of the OneTEAM Method™ is built on collaboration and teamwork. The Method merely helps teams to understand why and how they should collaborate. As tempted as you might be to force success upon your organization, resist the urge to make such an attempt. Buy-in from every level should make the implementation, while not easy, at least somewhat natural and more even handed. Forcing people, processes or technologies into situations or places in which they don't fit will get you nowhere really fast.

4. Build A Virtuous Cycle of Collaboration

When we talk about building and maintaining a virtuous circle of collaboration, it is only the latter (maintaining the circle) that will guarantee long-term success. Allow old habits and mindsets to creep back into the Sales/Marketing relationship and you will find yourself precisely back where you started.

To avoid slipping back into the bad habits that hindered Sales and Marketing departments from collaborating in the first place I highly recommend that organizations consider installing a dedicated person or team responsible for improving and maintaining Sales+Marketing Collaboration. My own research shows that such a resource is significantly more common in organizations with growing revenues than it is in non-growth organizations. Also, sales force effectiveness is stronger in organizations in which both Sales and Marketing report to a single executive. It shows that the closer the ties are between Sales and Marketing, the higher their success rate.

Be extremely diligent when assigning the task of overseeing Sales+Marketing Collaboration to anybody in-house. Neutrality is extremely important; the CMO/VP of Marketing or the CSO/VP of Sales shouldn't feel as though an internal stakeholder with their own vested interests is dictating to them. Keep in mind also that lower ranking people often don't feel comfortable expressing their true opinions and ideas to senior executives. They fear that too much limelight could be a CLM, career-limiting move" for them.

Finally, remember that the customer, of course, is also a member of the collaborative circle. Customers on the buyer's journey are looking for advisors, but they are also looking for collaborators. In a collaborative workplace, one in which Sales and Marketing are in every way consistent through every stage of customer interactions and there is a noticeable absence of territorial disputes (to which customers are extremely sensitive), will seem a more natural fit for these Buyer's Journey customers. The customer is the most important arbiter of successful Sales+Marketing Collaboration. All partnerships should aim to improve customer-facing aspects of both functions.

Attracting and retaining today's most desirable customers will become easier the longer you are able to maintain a virtuous circle of collaboration within your organization. When it comes to maintaining the collaborative environment and practices that typify the aligned organization, then the third element in the Trinity, namely 'Technology' becomes absolutely crucial.

So far, we have empowered the people, allowed them to help design their own processes and metrics, and enticed/compelled them to collaborate across the entire enterprize.

Now that the People are talking in constructive ways and the Processes are aligned in ways that make sure both departments are incentivized to collaborate like never before, the time has come to deploy a very different set of tools.

In order to make the practices we want to reinforce ubiquitous, transparent, and resilient, we'll need to turn to a tool that might surprise you considering my earlier critiques of the way that would-be collaborators have deployed it.

The tool is, as you might have guessed, technology.

After my frequent critiques of foolhardy technology implementations, it may seem as though I view technology vendors the same way the village folk viewed Frankenstein's monster, but this is not the case.

I am, believe it or not, an advocate for technology, but not if is deployed (as it so often is) for its own sake. To reinforce this point, let's take a closer look at an indispensable collaboration tool, one that helps the OneTEAM Method™ produce the kind of long-lasting and widely felt positive effects that I've highlighted throughout this book.

If you've ever been within earshot of a technology vendor, you've probably been told that a CRM system is the collaboration tool of choice. For this reason – and a handful of others – most would-be collaborators already have a CRM of some form or another in place. I'm not about to suggest that organizations should stop using their CRMs. What I am suggesting, however, is that they often are not the collaboration tools they are being touted as.

When sales reps are encouraged to speak candidly about the technologies they use, they frequently tell me that they regard CRMs not as sales support tools but, rather, as sales management tools. CRMs, I hear reps say, enforce control over Sales without offering any assistance in return. This is due to CRMs often-narrow focus on the sales lead generation and subsequent management process. This focus ignores broader collaboration issues, support processes that move predominantly in just one direction: from Marketing to Sales.

The standard approach seems to be for Marketing to create sales leads and pass them through the CRM to Sales for follow-up. Yes, sales reps can then leave feedback on whether, how and how well they followed up on the leads. Vendors have even created a new class of business jargon surrounding this process: Marketing Generated Leads (MGLs), Marketing Qualified Leads (MQLs), Sales Accepted Leads (SALs), Sales Closed Leads (SCLs), and many others. This one-way approach means that, more often than not, after the hand-off, Marketing has no idea what leads are working, or whether and how the sales team is following up on these leads.

Or, the opposite may also be the case.

During one of my invitation-only Executive Round Table breakfasts where I invite senior leaders from medium and large organizations to discuss their Sales+Marketing Collaboration practices the CMO of a large IT company told the group that in her organization the sales reps have become so accustomed to Marketing producing and nurturing the leads for them that they are now pushing back on Marketing if the leads are not for immediate opportunities.

In this organization it seems that Marketing has done such a good job that the sales reps have become spoilt and prefer to only take customers' orders, rather than doing any selling.

However, this is not what I call collaboration. Here, the pendulum has swung too far in another direction.

A bit more on CRMs. Granted, they have become more versatile over the past few years and they now include some, albeit limited, feedback loops. In recent years this has become particularly true when it comes to tracking the follow-up of sales leads, but it is still only a narrowly collaborative process. Some vendors have realized this shortcoming and have supplemented so-called 'collaboration tools' to their CRMs, but they mostly seem to me like Facebook for internal use, meaning that it can be very easy to spend a lot of time becoming lost in the various conversation streams without achieving a business outcome. Again, I have nothing against technology, but it must be implemented with the people (their strengths and their flaws alike) in mind, not merely with the processes.

In any case, there is more to Marketing than the generation of sales leads. What about other sales and marketing touch points? Wouldn't it make sense to create a feedback loop that also covers marketing content and collateral, campaigns, thought leadership pieces, white papers, brochures, videos, events, trade shows, web content and brand-building initiatives?

As my firm is not really a technology vendor, I am in a great position to help my clients select the technology solutions that best suit their needs. A couple of third-party technologies have frequently risen to the top as I have helped organizations build and maintain virtuous cycles of collaboration. I've found them so effective that they have pretty much become a permanent part of the OneTEAM Method™.

The first of these is a clever cloud application that helps organizations to make their team meetings substantially more effective. It works by allowing meeting participants to rate each other's contributions to the meeting. All this is very quick and painless. Once these ratings have been tabulated, each participant receives a report with their own score shown against both the anonymized lowest and the highest scores. I have noticed that the first time participants receive a low rating they tend to ignore it. However, if their colleagues continue to rate their contributions (or lack thereof) poorly, they tend to respond to this peer pressure by contributing in more substantial and constructive ways.

People are proud. Sales and marketing people are no exception to this rule. The app is able to leverage this pride in very clever and results-producing ways. After a short initial period during which users grow accustomed to using the technology, business meetings are notably improved.

The other technology that I have found particularly beneficial to would-be collaborators is a specialist cloud-based sales enablement and collaboration tool that directly integrates into most CRM systems and helps to enhance information exchange and collaboration between sales and marketing people. This cloud-based app has a whole host of useful features, but essentially is comprised of just three critical components:

1) An Online Repository

This is not intended to be something as complex as a content management system or even a document management system. Think of it more like an online filing cabinet with pre-labeled drawers and file folders. The key here is that Marketing controls all content that goes into the repository, which gives them an important measure of quality control. This, in turn, keeps the folders from becoming the kind of content black holes that I described earlier.

There is only one version of each piece of content, be it a document, a price list, a brochure, a video, a thought leadership piece, a white paper, a campaign, anything, and it is always the latest version. Sales reps are able to apply their own keywords to Marketing's online material, which allows them to search for and – importantly - to locate relevant material in a flash, whenever and wherever they need it. Since the app sits in the cloud, sales reps can access the service in the field or at the office via desktops and mobile devices.

2) A Ratings and Communications Engine

This empowers all members of the sales force to rate the quality of Marketing's content on a scale of 1 to 5, justify why they gave it that rating and make suggestions on how to improve it. In this way, all reps have an equal opportunity to provide feedback to Marketing, and Marketing can take the views and requirements of all the sales reps into consideration.

Marketing can then communicate through the app with the sales force and keep them informed about new initiatives and the changes they are making to respond to Sales' constructive feedback. This feature closes the feedback loop, making communication between Marketing and Sales truly bi-directional.

Crucially, it also encourages all sales reps to explain exactly *how* they are using the marketing-generated content in their daily interactions with prospects or customers. The value of this information cannot be overstated, especially in terms of speeding up ramp-up time for underperforming reps and new hires, and I am stunned by how few organizations are letting this information slip through their fingers. Your top reps' valuable sales know-how is walking out your front doors every night and, if these reps change jobs, that knowledge is lost to you forever. If they happen to move on to one of your competitors, that knowledge represents a substantial threat to your business. Knowing how your top reps are using content to win customers ensures that sales know-how stays within your organization, even when you lose one of your top performers.

3) A Management Dashboard

Through an executive dashboard management can see whether and how often individuals are making use of their opportunity to collaborate. Executives can pinpoint exactly who the team players are versus the lone wolves, and can manage each of them accordingly. It also provides data to better construct and monitor sales compensation plans and incentive structures.

As mentioned, the cloud app integrates seamlessly with most CRM systems and can be scaled up and down quickly to cater to any number of users in response to changing business environments. We even find that organizations are using it as a low-cost and quick-to-set-up portal for their indirect sales forces, and even for their resellers and distributors.

Now that we've got all the People, the Processes, and the Technologies in place, we have all the tools we need to build and maintain the virtuous cycle of collaboration. The symptoms of poor Sales+Marketing Collaboration should be starting to disappear, and collaborative practices should be starting to take their places. The last step in the OneTEAM Method™ ensures that the symptoms of misalignment don't return and that the collaborative practices you've worked hard to foster in your organization remain in place permanently.

1. Content Repository	2. Ratings & Feedback Engine	2. Management Dashboard
• Quick and easy for Sales reps to access the right content when they need it and wherever they are • Keeps Sales reps up to date, informed and effective on the road • Helps new reps to access the information to ramp up faster	• Fosters stronger Sales+Marketing collaboration • Improves both the quality and the effectiveness of Sales and Marketing content • Extracts valuable sales know-how from high performers for all reps to leverage	• Monitors the progress of team collaboration • Provides deeper executive insight through real-time data and reports • Identifies hidden trends and challenges • Enables better quality decision making

5. Maintain Collaboration Quality

I frequently talk about building and maintaining a virtuous cycle of collaboration in the same breath, but they are two separate steps in the Method, and the reason for this is simple. Building a collaborative cycle is obviously an important step in the collaborative journey, but only maintaining that cycle will guarantee long-term success. Allow old habits and mindsets to creep back into the Sales/Marketing relationship and you will find yourself precisely back where you started.

Well, if you consider how many people leave and how many new people join your organization each year it is not hard to see how over time things may not remain as collaborative as you would like.

I recommend that your HR team draws up an onboarding program for new employees that outlines the principles of the OneTEAM Method™ and what behavior is valued and even expected "around here".

To avoid slipping back into the bad habits that hindered Sales and Marketing departments from collaborating in the first place I highly recommend that organizations consider installing a dedicated person or team responsible for maintaining and improving Sales+Marketing Collaboration. My own <u>research</u> shows that such a resource is significantly more common in organizations with growing revenues than it is in non-growth organizations. This could be as simple as a single executive to which both Sales and Marketing report. My research also shows that sales force effectiveness is stronger in organizations with just such a dedicated executive, further strengthening the case for closer ties between Sales and Marketing at all organizational levels.

Be extremely diligent when assigning the task of overseeing Sales+Marketing Collaboration to anybody in-house. Neutrality is extremely important; the CMO/VP of Marketing or the CSO/VP of Sales shouldn't feel as though an internal stakeholder with their own vested interests is dictating to them. Keep in mind also that lower ranking people often don't feel comfortable expressing their true opinions and ideas to senior executives. They fear that too much limelight could be a 'CLM' (i.e. a 'career-limiting move') for them.

Finally, remember that the customer, of course, falls inside of the collaborative cycle. Customers on the buyer's journey are looking for advisors, but they are also looking for collaborators. A collaborative workplace, one in which Sales and Marketing are in every way consistent through every stage of customer interactions and there is a noticeable absence of territorial disputes (to which customers are extremely sensitive), will seem a more natural fit for these Buyer's Journey customers.

Regular check ups are an important part of maintaining your body's health, and the same can be said for the financial wellbeing of your organization.

I recommend ongoing check ups that assess the state of collaborative practices and address any sore spots that have popped up. My team and I perform dozens of these check ups every year, and many of my clients report that this ongoing work is a crucial part in their ongoing collaborative strategy.

Chapter Takeaway

Whether you are taking the first step of your collaborative journey or the last one, my team and I will be happy to help you through the steps OneTEAM Method steps that I have outlined above and ensure that you obtain the results that you are looking for. What's more, we will make sure these results last.

Peter Strohkorb

Chapter 20:
Reaping The Rewards

Let's briefly review where the successful implementation of the OneTEAM Method™ can take your organization. The vision for the OneTEAM Method™ is to create a world in which Sales and Marketing work harmoniously together as one, each one helping the other to get to, and to consistently remain at, their peak levels of performance.

So, as we have established, the OneTEAM Method™ is about facilitating People Collaboration. Admittedly, that is a pretty vague term in the eyes of most executives, perhaps with the exception of the head of HR. Very few CEOs that I know will approve funding for any new strategic initiative without at least a basic appreciation of the expected business returns, the financial outcomes, the return on investment (ROI) and the anticipated time to results.

What can OneTEAM Method™ collaborators expect?

Our slogan **"Collaboration. Growth. Success."** is built on these elements:

- up to 27% more sales revenue (because salespeople will spend more of their time selling, not creating their own marketing collateral)

- up to 36% greater gross profit(as Marketing will create more of the collateral that salespeople actually use)

- up to 23% higher lead conversion rates (as the right kind of collateral will finally accelerate sales velocity)

- up to 33% faster ramp-up for new sales reps (because better collaboration attracts higher performing talent)

- lower technology risk (as improved collaboration helps people to understand why they should use the technology and boosts technology utilization and end-user compliance)

- lower organizational risk (as organizations retain and leverage the personal know-how of their top sales performers)

- improved team morale (because Marketing will enjoy a better relationship with Sales, and vice versa)

Most senior executives I know are first and foremost interested in the financial benefits of any new solution. So, let's take a look at how the OneTEAM Method™ performs in this context.

Achievable Financial Outcomes

I have seen the OneTEAM Method™ deliver revenue growth from as little as 2.7% to as high as 24%. This is not taking into account the boosting effect that the OneTEAM Method™ can have on third-party point solutions that I identified earlier in this book. Further, this does not include the impact of a more collaborative, positive and enjoyable work environment, one in which staff is happy, supportive and being supported. Most importantly, they're not thinking about leaving for the perceived greener pastures of perhaps more collaborative competitors. Staff turnover is reduced, and as any CFO will tell you, that factor represents a significant cost saving that goes straight to the bottom line.

Even those organizations that received relatively low financial returns (e.g. in the 2-3% ROI range) were happy because, while the percentages do not sound impressive by themselves, the absolute/total revenue amounts that they gained were in the millions of dollars, which was well in excess of what the deployment of the OneTEAM Method™ had cost them.

In fact, my team and I frequently exceed an ROI of 10 : 1 for our clients.

In other words, for every dollar that our clients give us to help them build a more collaborative organization, we give them ten dollars back in productivity gains.

In the process of deploying the OneTEAM Method™ our clients also learn something important about their business and their people. This kind of in-depth understanding of your employees and the ways in which they can be encouraged to work together for the better of the whole organization may not have a hard dollar figure attached to it, but the so-called 'soft benefits' should also play a part in the ROI of the OneTEAM Method™ that take your teams away from an ingrained silo mindset to initial alignment and then all the way to true team collaboration.

Just like the bank that started off wondering why their sales and marketing people should work together at all, or the large pharmaceutical company that had multiple specialist reps calling on the same doctors, or the multinational manufacturer with centralized marketing based in China trying to support a regional sales force across culturally diverse countries like China, Japan, Malaysia, Korea and Australia. Or the globally well-known not-for-profit organization whose new local CEO had enormous initial trouble getting the salespeople and the marketers in her organization to collaborate, all kinds of organizations and the people within them received untold benefits from the choosing the OneTEAM Method™.

In summary, the OneTEAM Method™ delivers business results for all stakeholders:

For your Customers:

Your organization becomes one that your customers want to do business with. They recognize you as:

- A trusted brand
- A reliable business partner
- A competent advisor
- A competitively priced vendor
- A consistently high performer
- A valuable customer experience

For your Marketing Team:

Better alignment and deeper collaboration with Sales, resulting in:

- Less effort wasted on content that the sales team does not use (i.e. more effective utilization of Marketing resources)
- Greater recognition from the sales team of Marketing's contribution to results
- Better decision-making due to more complete and up-to-date information
- Less scrutiny of the Marketing budget due to improved performance and the more positive perspective of the sales team on Marketing's more actively supportive role

For your Sales Force:

More effective support from Marketing to help differentiate the organization from its competitors and to achieve sales targets:

- Accelerate sales velocity
- Retain high sales margins
- Reduce discounting
- Un-stick stuck sales
- Boost performance of the average sales performers

For your C-Suite Executives:

A future-proof organization with:

- Forecasts achieved
- More revenue
- Higher profits
- Lower risk
- Less staff turnover
- Improvement in morale
- More resilient and responsive teams
- A work environment that attracts top performing-talent

Chapter Takeaway

The business benefits of the OneTEAM Method are both tangible and intangible. In previous chapters, I have tried to quantify the tangible benefits in dollar terms because that is what drives business.

The intangible benefits of job satisfaction, a supportive work environment and team collaboration make for an altogether nicer place to work. As most of us tend to spend more than a third of our working days at work, isn't that also something that is worth investing in?

Peter Strohkorb

Chapter 21:
Prevention Is Better Than Cure

So far, we have only spoken about curing a pre-existing problem, i.e. applying the OneTEAM Method™ to help sales and marketing teams to work more effectively together again and to improve mutual support. There is, however, an additional reason for organizations to deploy the OneTEAM Method™: to prevent collaborative issues from becoming a problem in the first place.

The problems surrounding poor Sales+Marketing Collaboration develop as businesses grow and as the teams become more dispersed, both geographically and organizationally. There is really no sense in waiting for the problem to occur only to then attempt to fix it after the fact. There is, however, a lot to be said about heading off a potential business problem in the early stages of its growth.

As a business grows, the OneTEAM Method™ helps to put the elements in place to put it on the right track right from the start. One of our clients is an Australian arm of a global not-for-profit organization. Their new CEO came to us wanting the business to become more commercially sustainable. We joked that they had hitherto perhaps taken the term "not-for-profit" a bit too literally.

While conducting our OneTEAM Method™ Opportunity Analysis, we discovered that the organization had been getting by without any real marketing to speak of. When we started to take a closer look, it became clear that the same was true of the sales function Most of the organization's past success had come from the heroic efforts of a small number of individuals. There was no cohesive planning or strategy in place, and it didn't appear that there ever had been. As we discovered, the prevailing attitude of the staff was, "We work for a not-for-profit organization so we don't do any selling around here." The CEO agreed with our findings and liked what we had uncovered in the Opportunity Assessment phase, and she decided to go ahead with rolling out the OneTEAM Method™ across the organization. We implemented the method in a combination of online and face to face sessions and were able to complete the project within a seven month time frame, including the 360 Degree Opportunity Assessment and the OneTEAM Method™ implementation itself.

Right from the start, the method helped them come to grips with which collateral they already had in contrast to what they needed. We then helped them to understand how they could better support each other and build a more sustainable not-for-profit business.

The CEO made sure that the OneTEAM Method™ built on her foundations of an effective organizational structure, updated job descriptions and a new incentive scheme. This combination proved extremely effective in turning the business around and putting it on a commercially sustainable footing.

As we all know, an ounce of prevention is worth a pound of cure, and this is nowhere more true than in the world of collaborative enterprize. Organizations that find themselves in strong expansion mode and those that are about to open sales offices that are geographically separated from head office are strongly encouraged to consider leveraging the OneTEAM Method™ pro-actively.

Chapter Takeaway

Those who apply the OneTEAM Method™ preventatively are empowered to avoid the Sales/Marketing disconnect before it even begins to rear its ugly head.

Peter Strohkorb

Chapter 22:
The High Cost of Doing Nothing

Even though this chapter is the last in the book, it is perhaps the most important in terms of the messages that I wanted to send out when I wrote this book.

For a variety of reasons, many organizations procrastinate when it comes to making decisions, particularly when those decisions involve financial investment and/or are accompanied by any form of change. Many executives seem to think that by delaying the 'go' decision they delay spending and risk as well. Those who delay forget that there is significant risk in doing nothing.

Below are some points for you to consider when you are facing an important decision in your business life. Each of these has an inherent dollar value associated with them. As you will see, sitting on your hands may well be more expensive than you might think:

- Hanging on to inefficient business processes and procedures is wasteful
- Delaying the realization of business benefits is not smart
- Muddling through with the status quo is not innovative

- Getting by with quick fix 'Band-Aid' solutions is unsustainable
- Accepting an atmosphere of mutual blame and finger-pointing that leads to poor staff morale is unproductive
- Leaving the corporate sales know-how and the modus operandi of your top sales performers solely in their heads without using it to improve your average sales performers is foolish and risky

The OneTEAM Method™ is very simple. It is designed to lift both sales revenue and profitability by showing each team how to better support the other. It's the right decision for today's forward-thinking organizations.

Chapter Takeaway

Having spoken at length about both the tangible and the less tangible benefits of the OneTEAM Method it is timely to remind busy executives of the fact that there is a business cost in *not* making a decision. Unfortunately, it seems that many organizations suffer from the 'do nothing' syndrome where analysis paralysis, deferment, procrastination and deliberation are the orders of the day.

Leadership is about making good decisions, decisively.

Let us go forward and be leaders.

Peter Strohkorb

A Final Rally Cry

There is another, perhaps corporate-political, point to be made here.

Consider the following points:
- The problem of ineffective or non-existent Sales+Marketing Collaboration is ubiquitous and undeniable
- If there's one thing that all the experts agree on it's that something must be done
- Despite how much we know about a) the existence and b) the urgency of the problem, strategies and point solutions have been almost entirely ineffective

If you are the head of Sales or the head of Marketing, this problem presents you with something of an opportunity. What better way to demonstrate your leadership and problem-solving skills to the CEO?

Rather than saying something defeatist like "Oh well, it is what it is" (or words to that effect) why not grab the opportunity to shine with both hands, stand up and say "For the good of the organization, I am willing to do something about this, and I invite my counterpart to join me in taking this initiative!"

Such a statement – especially when it is followed by concerted action – will establish you as a man or woman of action, and you have forced your counterpart's hand into accepting your plan. Again, you come out looking like a leader who is taking the initiative. Such a move could do wonders for your career.

Think about it.

No, even better still:

Go ahead and DO it.

The End

or maybe a new beginning...?

ABOUT THE AUTHOR

With 20 years of experience in executive B2B sales and marketing positions for some of the largest corporations on the planet, such as SONY, 3M, Canon and CSC, Peter Strohkorb has a history of showing businesses how to succeed in a broad range of competitive markets.

Today, Peter is CEO at Peter Strohkorb Consulting International, a specialist business consulting firm with offices in Australia and the USA that consults medium and large organizations on how to boost their Sales and Marketing productivity through closer collaboration.

Peter Strohkorb Consulting International now offers the OneTEAM Method, a structured Sales and Marketing Productivity Framework to help your Sales force and your Marketing resources work together as one team, to boost sales and lift staff morale.

Peter Strohkorb works with CEOs, Sales and Marketing executives, and with their customers, to enable a more collaborative working environment to the benefit of your entire organization.

Peter is a guest lecturer in the Executive MBA program of the Sydney Business School and in the MBA Master Class at the University of Wollongong, Australia.

Peter has appeared in press, radio, on stage and online and he is a recognized speaker, presenter and author in his field.

He is also a paid up member of the National Speakers Association and holds qualifications in Marketing and Management from the Macquarie Graduate School of Management (MGSM) in Sydney, Australia.

CONTACT

Email: admin@peterstrohkorbconsulting.com
Web: http://www.peterstrohkorbconsulting.com
Web: http://www.peterstrohkorb.com
LinkedIn: au.linkedin.com/in/peterstrohkorbsalesmarketing/en
Twitter: @pstrohkorb

42155425R00166

Made in the USA
Lexington, KY
10 June 2015